MW01291496

The Art of Attraction

Why the law of attraction is the most important natural law in your life

ELSE BYSKOV, MA & BA

YOUR THOUGHTS ARE MAGNETIC AND YOU ATTRACT PEOPLE, CONDITIONS AND OCCURRENCES IN YOUR LIFE ACCORDING TO YOUR PREVAILING THOUGHT PATTERNS.

The Art of Attraction © Else Byskov, 2009

By the same author:
"Death Is an Illusion" (Paragon House Publishers, USA 2002)
"Der Tod Ist eine Illusion" (Martinus Verlag, Germany 2006 and BOD, De 2014)
"La Muerte Es Una Ilusión" (Corona Borealis, Spain 2011)
"Døden er en illusion", (BOD, DK 2011)
"Loven for tiltrækning" (Kosmologisk Information, DK 2008 and BOD, DK 2011)
"The Beginning Is Near" (Create Space, USA 2016)
"Ti nye måder at se verden på – På forkant af et nyt verdensbillede" (BOD, DK 2010)
"The Undiscovered Country – A Non-religious Look at Life after Death" (Create Space, USA 2010)
"Glad Mad – en vegetarisk kogebog uden dikkedarer" (BOD, DK 2010)
"Fod på Andalusien – 40 udflugter med indlagt vandring i den sydspanske natur". (BOD, DK 2011)
"On Foot on Andalucía – 40 hiking excursions in Southern Spain" (Create Space, USA, 2014)
"Fod på Andalusien 2 – 25 udflugts og vandreture øst og nordøst for Málaga" (BOD, DK 2014)
"Fod på Andalusien 3 – 25 udflugts og vandreture vest og nordvest for Málaga", BOD, DK, 2016)
"Zu Fuß in Andalusien - 40 Wanderausflüge in Südspanien." (BOD, De 2015)
"The Downfall of Marriage - The Great Transformation within" (Create Space, 2016)

Websites of the author:
www.newspiritualscience.com
www.elsebyskov.com
www.deathisanillusion.dk (in four languages)

Part I   *page*   *7*

The Law of Attraction and the Creation of Fate

Your life is your own responsibility
Examples of appropriate attraction

Part II   *104*

The Law of Attraction during the Reincarnation Process and after the Death of the Physical Body

A corpse is a worn out instrument
We <u>are</u> our vibration
The unpleasant good
Destinations in the spiritual world
Spiritual matter shapes itself according to our thoughts
Weeding in the thought sphere
The road of life

Part I

The Law of Attraction and the Creation of Fate

1. Introduction

The existence of a law of attraction may come as a surprise to many people, but it is beyond doubt that such a natural law exists. The law of attraction decrees that energies on the same wavelength attract each other and that energies on dissimilar wavelengths repel each other. We know the law from the transmission of radio-, television-, and mobile telephone waves, but very few people realize that the law also affects our daily lives through the magnetism that our thoughts hold.

The law of attraction is active in your life around the clock whether you realize it or not. The day you realize that you can cooperate with this natural law in order to obtain the things and conditions you want in your life can be the most important day in your entire life. The workings of the law of attraction are absolutely fantastic, fabulous and amazing. Working with this law can make you the master of life instead of its slave. It will show you that you are the one who decides what happens in your life with respect to whom you meet, which job you hold, your health, your prosperity, your fate – indeed your whole happiness. You may think that I'm exaggerating, but it is impossible to exaggerate the importance of this law. And there is not a shadow of proof that the law does not work.

This book will explain how and why the law of attraction works and it will also provide you with all the proof you need. Also it will give you the necessary tools to make your life unfold in the ways you most desire.

My own life has been one long string of proof that the law of attraction works, but it was only when I came across the work of the Danish intuitive Martinus that I realized that such a law existed. And then, when a few years later I came across Abraham, the group of spiritual beings channeled by Esther Hicks, it became clear to me in all its amazing glory that you can actively make use of this law to obtain what you want. The law of attraction works because your thoughts are magnetic and attract the things you think about.

I think that the first time I realized that there was power in my thoughts was when my then 14-year-old son and I had gone on a canoeing trip to Sweden. We didn't have a lot of money, so as we were walking through the town of Växjö I thought that it would be great, if there would be 100 Swedish kroner sitting in a cash machine, which I could just take. I had hardly finished the thought, when we passed a cash machine and when I looked, there actually *was* a 100 kroner bill sitting there. It was so unexpected, and I was both surprised and pleased when I took the money. We soon spent it, but I never forgot the peculiar episode.

Seen in retrospect I can in all sincerity say that everything I have wanted in life has come true. I may have had wishes, that I had not nurtured for very long and which I had forgotten before they became reality, but all the important things that I wanted have come true.

When I had graduated from university in Spanish and English philology I lived in Aarhus, Denmark and was unemployed and poor as a church mouse. My secret dream was to meet a well-to-do man, whom I could fall in love with. I did not want to marry for money, but to seek love where money abounded. I visualized myself living in a house that had a view over a lake. A year and a half after my visualization I had married a dentist and had moved to Viborg, where we had a view over the lake Nørresø.

Another dream I had was to move to Spain. I had majored in Spanish and was in love with the thought of living in a house with a view over the Mediterranean. I also saw myself speaking Spanish like a native all the time. And I said to myself many times as I looked out across Nørresø: I want Nørresø replaced with the Mediterranean. In 1990 we immigrated to Spain and have lived there ever since. And yes, we have a magnificent view of the Mediterranean and I speak Spanish like a native.

When we moved to Spain, I had a dream of getting a job in the world of business. I had worked as a secondary school teacher for 11 years when we emigrated, and I wanted to try something with more excitement and glamour. I could see myself working as an interpreter at business meetings, traveling all over the world, checking in and out of hotels, stepping on and off planes, attending trade fairs and in general being smart and in control. A year after we had moved to Spain, a man turned up and offered me precisely the job I had visualized. It wasn't that I had applied for a job, no; this man just turned up out of the blue and offered me a job with all the ingredients I had wished for.

My husband had opened a dental practice and after a few years he had more patients than he himself could attend to. We thought that it would be great with another dentist, but we didn't dare advertise, because we weren't sure if there would be enough patients for two. One day my husband received a letter from a young dentist, who would like to move to Spain, and he asked if he could come by to say hello. We were happy for him to do that, and we soon agreed to offer him the job. Much to our surprise he had come all the way to Spain from Denmark just to see us. There were many other Danish dentists down here, whom he could meet, but he only saw us. We employed him and he moved to Spain – and there were enough patients. They just came.

As long back as I can remember I have had a vague idea that one day I would write a book. But my book shouldn't be an ordinary book, but a book with a new and different content. I had almost forgotten about my book project when one day in 1995 a book about the Danish intuitive Martinus literally fell into my hands. I had never before heard about the man and had been an atheist for 30 years, when Martinus entered my life with a vengeance. I threw myself upon his books in the manner of a starved crocodile and was completely taken aback by his totally logical world picture. It was so overwhelming, so huge, so surprising and so fantastic, that I had to tell somebody about it. This resulted in my book "Death is an Illusion. A Logical Explanation Based on Martinus' Worldview". I wrote the book in English in less than 6 months and it was published in the USA in 2002.

One would now suppose that we were beginning to get it and to realize that there was power in our thoughts. But no – it was only when I, after 9 years of business life, had had enough of traveling, trade fairs, planes and hotels and decided to take a break, that it became obvious, that there was something unexpected going on.

Through my study of Martinus' work I had become very interested in the spiritual side of life and decided that I would walk a part of El Camino, the old pilgrim road in Northern Spain. I wanted to walk alone and seek contemplation, peace and insight.

I took the bus from Almuñecar to Burgos and was now about to embark on my long walk. It was around 7 PM when I arrived in Burgos, and I had to find the municipal refuge, which was somewhere out there and a long way from the bus station. I had hardly stepped out from the bus station, when an elderly man approached me and asked if I was a pilgrim. Under the circumstances I had to say yes to that, although I had never thought of myself as such. *"I'll show you the way to the refuge",* he said and he took me all the way there. It was a long way away, at least half an hour's walk and I would never have found it myself. When I had thanked him and had been shown a bed, I thought that this was a good beginning of my pilgrimage. The help I had needed had materialized just through my wanting to find the way and without my needing to ask anybody for it. But that was only the beginning.

The next day I walked out of Burgos early in the morning. It was in November and it was cold – about 2 degrees Celsius. I had more or less planned that I would walk 26 km. the first day, as I figured that that was what I could handle. It got mild and sunny later in the day, and I walked happily along with my rucksack. At intervals I rested and relaxed in the sun. Around mid afternoon I was beginning to get tired, but I was nowhere near refuges or villages.

Suddenly I spotted a young man, who looked as if he were waiting for me. As soon as I was within earshot, he said to me in Spanish: *"Now you have walked 26 km. I have a car standing over there and if you want, I can take you to Castrojeriz. There is already another pilgrim waiting in the car"*. Ok, I thought, funny that he should know about my planned 26 km. And fortunate, that he was right there, because I was getting quite tired. I was then driven to Castrojeriz in style and was shown the way to the refuge.

On the way to the refuge I passed a lovely, new hotel and thought that I would like to sleep there. But this was a pilgrimage, and not a luxury holiday, so I looked for the refuge. When I found it and looked in I lost heart, because it was miserable, cold, damp and none too clean. I couldn't make myself spend the night there, so instead I went to a hostal, where I had a primitive, but heated room for 16 €. Before showering I felt like a cup of coffee and went down to the bar to get a "café con leche". It was the hostess who was attending the bar and she asked me, *"Are you going to take a shower?"* *"Yes"*, I said. *"Well, then go and get your things, because we don't have any hot water today. I'll give you another room at the same price."* She then led me along the street and great was my surprise when we entered the lovely, new hotel, where I was given a wonderful room with heating, shower, tub and TV. When I was soaking in the tub I was thinking that it was a bit mysterious that I just had to think of something and then it would happen.

And it went on like that. If I had taken the wrong way, immediately someone would appear who could point me in the right direction, if I wanted company, immediately somebody came and sat next to me so that we could chat, if I needed massage on my sore limbs, there would be a notice about massage at the next place to sleep, if I was hungry, people at the refuge would offer me a hot meal. But the greatest experience was the one with the blue bread van.

One morning, after having spent the night in Calzadilla de la Cueza, which is a fairly miserable village in the middle of extensive plough lands, I realized that I had run out of bread. I asked at the inn, if I could buy some bread, but strangely enough none was available. I then asked if there were any shops nearby or on the way to Sahagún, but I was told that there wasn't any. Well, I thought, then I just have to leave the bread supply to Providence. And with that thought I stepped out onto the sunny Camino. I walked through several small villages, where there were neither bars nor shops, and around 1 o'clock I was beginning to get hungry. But I had nothing but some cheese spread and no bread to spread it on. In the village of Moratinos I had a sudden impulse to sit down on a bench, and I had hardly sat down, when a brand new blue bread van drove straight into my field of vision and stopped right next to me. I could hardly believe my own eyes when I stepped up to the van to buy bread. The bread I had wanted was delivered right at my feet at the precise moment I needed it. It was at the very moment when I saw the blue bread van that it finally dawned on me in all its fabulous glory that something was going on that was more fantastic than I had ever dared imagine.

What I was witnessing was the law of attraction in action, only I didn't realize it at the time. But how is it possible? How does it work? That is what this book is all about.

2. Thoughts and the Laws of Nature

Thoughts Are "Something" that Can Be Measured

Your thoughts are the key to what you attract in life, so let us begin with thoughts. Some people may think that thoughts don't matter and that it is of no consequence, what we think, because thoughts are completely immaterial, they are just "nothing". But it is simply not so. Today it is a fact that thoughts are measurable. By placing electrodes on a person's head, we can measure the degree of thought activity taking place. Thoughts are measurable, and something that is measurable is not "nothing". Thoughts are "something", and this something" is so material that we can measure it with modern measuring equipment.

The Electromagnetic Spectrum

Thoughts are essentially a form of electromagnetic radiation. One can say that it is a kind of non-physical type of matter; we call it non-physical because we can neither see nor touch it, it is invisible and intangible. But in spite of being invisible and intangible, still it is there, it is something. We know it is there because we can measure it. Furthermore it is a type of matter that can hold or carry information.

Martinus often denominates this non-physical type of matter as ray-formed matter, precisely because it consists of invisible waves and rays. Today ray-formed matter is mostly denominated as electromagnetic radiation, and nowadays there will hardly be a single well-informed person who would claim that invisible matter does not exist. Because everybody who uses radio, television and mobile phones knows that it does. When we watch television, listen to the radio or talk on our mobile phones information is transported through the air at the speed of light via electromagnetic radiation. We can then receive this information in our various devises, which transform it into something we can see or hear, but the "medium of transport" itself, i.e. the electromagnetic waves, is completely immaterial – we can neither see, hear nor feel the electromagnetic waves.

Electromagnetic radiation is all the different waves and rays which in mainly invisible form surround us all over the globe. There are waves provided by nature, such as radiation from the earth, radiation from space, ultraviolet and infrared rays from the Sun, but there are also rays produced by us humans, such as radio waves, microwaves, radar waves, television waves, waves from mobile phones, X-rays, gamma waves etc.

These rays and waves are floating all around us, and they help us communicate, they entertain us, and they are used in various kinds of medical treatment. All these rays and waves operate on different wavelengths and frequencies, and they have been "organized" by science in the so-called electromagnetic spectrum. The waves have been classified according to their length, so that the longest waves have been placed to the left of the spectrum (long radio waves) and the shortest waves (gamma waves) have been placed to the right.

The electromagnetic spectrum can be pictured like this:

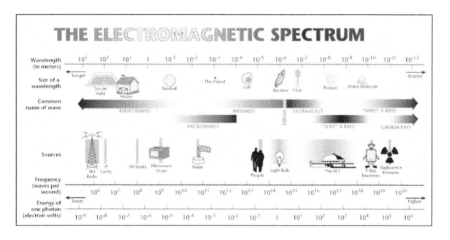

The electromagnetic spectrum, including radio waves, micro waves, infrared rays, visible light, ultraviolet rays, soft and hard x-rays and gamma rays. The wavelength is read in the line at the top and by way of illustration things are shown underneath, whose size corresponds to the wave length. That means that long radio waves have a length of 10 meters raised to the second power or are as long as a football field. The length of the micro waves, we use in our micro oven, are the size of a base ball and the length of the waves, that we humans emit, are shorter than the diameter of a cell. The shortest waves are gamma waves, which are so short, that their diameter is less than that of a water molecule: less than 10 to the power of minus 11. The frequency, i.e. the number of waves per second, can be seen on the second line from the bottom, while the energy of the photons of the wave can be seen on the bottom line. The part of the spectrum pictured here is only a segment – the arrows suggest that the wavelengths can be both longer and shorter, just as the frequencies can be higher and lower. Indeed there are no known limits no neither wavelengths nor frequencies.

(Source: Micro Worlds at
www.lbl.gov/MicroWorlds/ALSTool/EMSpec/EMSpec2.html)

Also the light, which we can see, forms part of the electromagnetic spectrum, but visible light only makes up a very small fraction of the spectrum, placed between the ultraviolet and infrared rays. The eye can perceive visible light, but all the other rays, i.e. by far the larger part of the spectrum, is invisible. This means that we are surrounded by invisible rays and waves wherever we go, and it also means that today it has become clear that invisible and intangible "matter" exists. Invisible rays and waves exist, they are not "nothing", but "something", and we know that as we make use of them every day. For that same reason it is no use claiming that the world only consists of what can be seen and weighed. A large and real aspect of the world is immaterial in the sense that we cannot see it, touch it or grab it. It is quite simply outside the range of our ability of perception. But we know it exists, because it can be measured and used by us humans.

If we look at the drawing of the electromagnetic spectrum, we see two people a little to the right of the middle. The people have been placed at the precise place of the spectrum where their measurable radiation lies with respect to wavelength and frequency, i.e. at a wavelength of 10 to the power of minus 5 and between the frequencies of 10 to the power of 13 and 14. That means that people emit electromagnetic waves or vibrations. This emission is partly determined by the temperature and physical / chemical composition of the body, but as our thoughts are also electromagnetic waves, the quality of our thoughts plays a role as to the wavelength we emit. Our choice of thoughts influences the wavelength we emit. Or said in a different way: the whole of our psyche, i.e. the way we think, react and feel, is decisive for the wavelength we emit. All people emit a specific wavelength and because similar wavelengths attract each other, we will automatically be attracted to other people whose wavelength is similar to our own.

For that reason we sometimes say that we are "on wavelength" with other people and consequently feel attracted to them. This is not just a saying, but a factual phenomenon defined by the law of attraction. We are quite simply attracted to people whose psyche operates on wavelengths that match our own. We then feel that we have a lot in common with these people; we feel that they are easy to talk to and we can easily relate to them.

On the other hand we feel repelled by people whose psyche is very different from our own, and we normally do not want to have anything to do with them. We all know this phenomenon from our everyday lives, where we like to meet up with like-minded people, but would rather not get involved with groups of people with whom we have nothing in common. This attraction and repulsion, which we sense, is not a chance phenomenon, but is determined by the attraction that similar wavelengths have on each other.

The Laws of Nature

The existence of invisible rays and waves also means that there necessarily has to be a natural law that defines the behavior of these waves. Such a law has to exist, because we live in a universe that is governed by laws. These natural laws are so exact and constant that we can "rely" on them. If we want to build a bridge, we can calculate how much concrete and iron is needed for the bridge, because we know which natural laws will affect the bridge. For instance we know the effect of the law of gravity, and because we do, we can calculate exactly how much material we need so that the bridge can carry the weight we need it to carry. The natural laws are so reliable and unwavering that we can send a man to the moon and bring him down again, simply because we know that the natural laws are always constant. When we know the natural laws, we can send a space ship into orbit around the Earth, because we can calculate how much fuel is needed for the space ship to get enough force to release itself from the gravitational field of the planet. It is a "simple" calculation, because we know that the effect of the natural laws is always constant. The law of gravity does not have one value today and another one tomorrow, and it does not have a specific value in China and another one in France. It is valid all over the globe, that if a man falls from a window on the 17. floor, then he'll hit the ground a few seconds later. There is no vacillation in the law of gravity and there is no vacillation in any of the other natural laws, which have been described by the science of physics. A natural law is a law, and a natural law is always valid.

Known Ways of Exploiting the Law of Attraction and Repulsion

It has been known to Mankind for more than 100 years that a natural law exists, which "dictates" that similar wavelengths attract each other. This has been known ever since Guglielmo Marconi in 1895 sent radio waves across his garden, thus taking the first step towards us being able to listen to the radio.

It is the law of attraction that determines that we can attract certain radio waves in our radio receiver. When we turn the buttons of the radio receiver, we tune the apparatus to a specific wave length. In this way we have "told" the apparatus, which radio waves on which wavelength and frequency we want to attract. This works, because the law of attraction and repulsion decrees that similar wavelengths attract each other. The law of attraction and repulsion is a natural law that we can count on, and it is not so, that it works on Sundays and not on Wednesdays, or that it works on odd dates and not on even dates. The law behaves like all other natural laws: **it always works and its working is constant and reliable.**

We can thank modern science and modern technological advances that it is possible for us to listen to the radio, watch television, have conversations via mobile phones, use radar and sonar and in general communicate far easier than only 30 years ago. A considerable part of this technological advance is based on our ability to exploit the possibilities determined by the law of attraction, precisely because we know that similar wavelengths attract each other. We know the law and have become good at exploiting it to our own advantage.

But modern science has in no way exhausted the possibilities inherent in the law of attraction. This law works in a whole series of fields that science has no actual knowledge about and about which it consequently cannot advice us. If we want to know more about what type of thoughts to think in order to best make use of the law of attraction and repulsion in the shaping of our fate and the achievement of our own happiness, it is no use that we go to the university and ask to be taught this discipline. It is no use, because an **Institute for the applied exploitation of the law of attraction and repulsion** does not exist. And when this knowledge is not to be found at the universities, then many people may think that there is no such knowledge; that such knowledge simply does not exist. But that is definitely not the case. Knowledge exists that lies way beyond what the universities of this planet can offer, and this knowledge is very, very useful to us. It is actually so useful that it would be both foolish and unwise if we did not accept it and apply it to our own lives.

The knowledge that I'm talking about is not a knowledge achieved through the study of books and scientific experiments. It is a knowledge that has come from spiritual sources, from "above", so to speak. It is a knowledge that has been revealed to selected persons on Earth, who, through a strong intuitive ability, have had access to the sea of knowledge that the universe also holds. These persons have, either through cosmic glimpses or permanent cosmic consciousness, been able to reveal aspects of the universal laws of life. In the next chapter we shall become acquainted with one of the greatest of all intuitives: the Danish mystic Martinus. We shall also look at the phenomenon Abraham and explain why it is of great value to merge the knowledge revealed by these two metaphysical sources.

3. Martinus and Abraham

In this chapter I shall present a short introduction to the great Danish intuitive Martinus and to the highly interesting phenomenon Abraham and explain why it is useful to let the two supplement each other. The law of attraction has recently come into focus through the DVD and book "The Secret" (2006) and also through the books and DVDs by Esther and Jerry Hicks, who channel Abraham. However, as far back as 1932 Martinus wrote extensively about the law of attraction, so it seems relevant to include Martinus' contributions in today's law of attraction forum, as his writings hold new, surprising aspects of the importance of the law. As Martinus is practically unknown, a thorough introduction to who he was is presented below.

Martinus

The fact that Denmark has produced such a great intuitive as Martinus must be the best kept secret of the country. Today (2009), 28 years after his death in March 1981, very few people have heard about Martinus and even fewer are acquainted with his unique work. We shall now take a look at who Martinus was.

Martinus was born at the small holding Moskildvad in Sindal, between Frederikshavn and Hjørring in the north of Jutland, Denmark, just around midnight between August 12 and 13 1890. His mother was unmarried and it is still being debated who Martinus´ father was. The mother was a house keeper at the manor house Christianshede, and it was possibly the lord of the manor, Lars Larsen, who was Martinus´ biological father. But in order to avoid a scandal it was, however, the foreman Michael Thomsen, who was proclaimed to be Martinus' father, and consequently the boy's full name was Martinus Thomsen. The mother could not have her "illegitimate" child with her at Christianshede, so shortly after the birth she had the boy adopted by her half brother and his wife, who owned the small holding where Martinus had been born.

These two simple, unread people agreed to bring up Martinus in spite of the fact that they were both well on in years and had 11 children themselves. Of these 11 children there were only two that still lived at home when Martinus was born – two boys of 3 and 5 respectively. In the small holding there was one large room, which was both dining room and bedroom. There were two beds, and the adoptive parents slept in one bed and the three boys in the other. From this room one entered a small kitchen, which then opened directly on to the stable (1).

Martinus grew up in these humble surroundings, and much of his childhood was spent herding cows and helping out on neighboring farms. He only had a rudimentary schooling, in which he learnt a bit of arithmetic, Danish, history and biblical knowledge. Already as a very young child he showed great intuitive understanding and he often disagreed in the way the priest interpreted the Bible. For instance, Martinus was told that he, as an "illegitimate" child, was cast out by God and that all children born outside marriage were eternally lost. In spite of his young age Martinus felt absolutely convinced that the priest was wrong. He did in no way feel that God was angry with him, on the contrary he had a very intense relationship to God and not a day went by when he did not pray to Providence.

Martinus 11 years old

As the foster parents could not afford to let Martinus study, he had to find a way to support himself, and he decided, when he was in his teens, that he wanted to be a dairyman. He worked as such at several dairies in Jutland and Fuenen and when he was in his mid twenties, he moved to Copenhagen.

In Copenhagen he had various jobs, both as a postman and a security guard, but he also kept working in the dairy business, and when he was in his late twenties, he was employed as a clerk at the diary Enigheden. At this point in time he was living in a rented room at Jagtvej 52 A, overlooking Nørrebros Runddel.

It was in this rented room that the most significant event of Martinus' life took place. The event took place on March 21st 1921, approximately 7 months after Martinus had turned 30. A book about meditation had found its way into Martinus´ hands and he now decided to follow the instructions of the book and sit down to meditate on the concept of God. He rolled down the blinds, blindfolded himself and sat down in his new wicker chair and concentrated his thoughts on God.

He had hardly started his meditation, when a white spot of light appeared to his inner vision. We will let Martinus himself tell about the event that was later called his cosmic baptism of fire. (2)

"According to the instructions in the book I had borrowed, one evening I tried to meditate on the concept of "God". And suddenly, without my knowing how, I found myself in a state, where it seemed to me that I was in the presence of something exceedingly elevated. A very small point of light appeared far off. For a moment it was gone. But in the next second it reappeared, but now much closer. Now I could see that the light emanated from a Christ-like being, whose details appeared in a blinding white light with blue details. The light was so intense and alive that it reminded me of the Roman candles we use around Christmas. Only the stars of the revelation were much, much smaller but much more numerous.

There was a pause, where I was in a kind of darkness, but then the form lit up the plateau anew. I looked straight into a form of fire. A Christ-like being of blinding sunlight now moved with his arms raised as if for hugging straight towards me. I was completely paralyzed. Without being able to move at all I stared right into the belt region of the shining being, which was now level with my eyes. But the form continued his forward movement; and in the next moment it walked straight into my own flesh and blood. A wonderful, sublime feeling took hold of me. The paralysis was over. The divine light, that had thus inhabited me, gave me the ability to look out over the world.

And look! Continents and seas, cities and countries, mountains and valleys were steeped in the light from my own interior. In the white light the Earth was transformed into" the kingdom of God".

The divine experience was over. Again I had before me the physical reality, the details of my room, the inferiority of my position. But "the kingdom of God" was still sparkling in my brain and in my nerves." (Martinus: On the Birth of My Mission, chapter 16).

The following day Martinus sat down again in his medita-tion chair and again he was surrounded by the divine light.

"I looked into a blue bright sky, which was then pulled aside wherewith a new and even brighter sky appeared, which was of such exuberantly blinding golden light and of such a fast vibrating matter, that I felt that I was at the height or top of what my organism and consciousness could bear. One single step, a single fraction of a second more, and the celestial wavelength would with the extreme power of lightning immediately have forced me out of all physical existence. But in the fractions of a second the revelation lasted I experienced a world of holiness, purity, harmony and perfection. I found myself in a sea of light. This was not, as in my first revelation, white as snow, but it had the color of gold. All details were golden fire. Through all of it small, golden threads were vibrating, which sparkled and scintillated here, there and everywhere. I felt that this was God's consciousness, his own sphere of thought. It was the matter, the omnipotence, the highest living force, through which the divine I governed and ruled oceans of worlds, milky ways and star cities, both in micro cosmos and in macro cosmos. I was quite spellbound. The divine fire vibrated inside me and outside of me, above me and below me". (Martinus: Ibid, chapter 17).

Martinus at 30. The picture was taken a few months after his cosmic baptism of fire

Martinus points out that this experience would have been of no importance to others than himself had it not left him in a permanent state of "access" to a sublime divine dimension with a pertaining sea of knowledge.

"A change had happened to my being. I had been born into a new world, had become conscious in a new body. And from that moment the world, which lies beyond all physical phenomena, had been permanently incorporated in my day consciousness. The golden light had left me in a state of conscious immortality and with the ability to see that only life exists, and that darkness and suffering are nothing but camouflaged love, and that the being of God is present in everything and everybody." (Martinus: Ibid, chapter 18).

After the cosmic baptism of fire it was so that Martinus had achieved what could be called permanent cosmic consciousness (3). He had "simply" attained permanent "access" to the sea of knowledge of the universe. From now on it was so that whenever Martinus concentrated his thoughts on a specific question, the answer came immediately, as a finished solution. The unlimited access that Martinus had to the cosmic sea of knowledge meant that there was no question that he could not answer. All the true facts and highest laws of life were revealed to him.

Now there might be somebody who would claim that this is all just something that Martinus has imagined and that it consequently has no value of truth, indeed, somebody might even claim that it is all a figment of the imagination or fantasy sprung from an inventive mind. But one can only claim that, when one has not read Martinus' work and consequently is ignorant about its contents. Because not even the most developed fantasy can come up with a complete, holistic world picture based on logic. If it were so simple that fantasy alone could do the trick, well, then the world literature would be full of world pictures. But it isn't and Martinus' work is to this day the most complete revelation of the mystery of life and the laws that govern the universe. It is an unequalled, completely unique work. It is an oeuvre that holds the keys to the universe.

It must be pointed out that Martinus, at the time when he had his cosmic baptism, never had studied anything; he was completely unread. When in spite of this he came to write a gigantic work on the laws and logic of life, it was based on the consciousness expansion that he experienced in 1921. He wrote practically every day from the time of his initiation until his death in 1981. It was to be an oeuvre of approximately 8000 pages comprising his main work "Livets Bog" ("The Book of Life", 7 volumes), the work "Det Evige Verdensbillede" ("The Eternal World Picture", 4 volumes), the books "Logic" and " On Funerals", 28 booklets, approximately 200 articles (45 of these have been published in the book "Collection of articles 1"), the posthumously published (2004) "The Intellectualized Christianity , plus 44 so-called symbols, which are colored drawings that in a beautiful visual form illustrate aspects of Martinus' world picture.

Martinus' work is living proof that it is possible to achieve profound knowledge about the laws of life without having studied.

The importance of the work of Martinus cannot be exaggerated – it is so great, so fantastic and so epoch-making that today we can hardly estimate what it will mean to future generations. Everything is there: the meaning of life, the solution to the mystery of life, from where we are coming and to where we are going, immortality as the logical premise for the evolution of life, reincarnation as the necessary foundation for the existence of all physical life forms, the laws and logic of the creation of fate and karma, the existence of the spiritual world as a prerequisite for the existence of the physical universe, the irrevocable existence of an intelligent creator, the power of prayer and the importance of thoughts, the mission of darkness, the importance of the law of attraction, the transformation of the sexual poles, the combination of the basic energies, the nature of the universe, the analysis of the "I" and much, much more.

Everything has been written with mathematical precision and logic, which appeals to the intellectual human being, whose ability to believe has degenerated to the degree that he or she can no longer be seduced by the magic of the religions. Martinus' work is spiritual nourishment for the modern, intellectual human being, who cannot accept to believe without being able to understand. It is spiritual nourishment for those who have lost the ability to believe and have a need to know the solution to the mystery of life. His work is meant to appeal to the intellect and does not, as previous spiritual revelations did, appeal to the feelings. This means that those who can still believe will not feel attracted to his work, as it has not been written for them. Martinus' work has been written for the atheists and non-believers who, through their accumulated life experiences during many incarnations, have reached a point where they are looking for answers to the meaning of life beyond what the materialistic sciences can offer. The law of attraction will see to it that those who are ready will become acquainted with Martinus' work. Because *"when the pupil is ready, the teacher will appear"*.

It must be underlined that Martinus' work is not an object of faith and that he doesn't want anybody to believe in his analyses. What he wants us to do is to study his work and then go out into the world to see, if what he says, does not coincide with what can be observed "out there". It is only through these comparative studies and through one's own accumulation of experience that Martinus' work can be of value.

It should also be pointed out that there is no association or sect around Martinus' work. That means there is no organization to join, no forms of ritual to carry out for those who are on wavelength with Martinus' thoughts. Martinus' thoughts are freely accessible to everybody as they belong to all of Mankind.

It lies outside the scope of this book to introduce Martinus' world picture, but the interested reader can find references to titles that do that in the notes (4).

Abraham

The phenomenon of Abraham is of an even later date than Martinus and has only been manifested from the first half of the 1980's. Abraham is a group of highly evolved spiritual (discarnate) beings that are channeled, which means made manifest in a form accessible to physical beings, through an American lady called Esther Hicks, married to Jerry Hicks.

How Esther Hicks became a channel for spiritual knowledge from the Abraham group shall be briefly outlined here.

When Esther got married to Jerry she was a completely blank page with regard to belief in or contact to a spiritual dimension. Jerry, on the other hand, had had spiritual interests ever since he was a young child, and he had been in and out of several religious creeds. He had also participated in several mediumistic séances, in which, among other things, a so-called ouija board was used.

Through the ouija board Jerry had become convinced that contact to "the other side" could be established, as he received valuable advice via the board about what he should do in order to learn more. However, he soon dropped the board again, as the value of the information turned out to be very inconstant. One day, when Jerry was in a library, he came across a book by Seth, the spiritual entity that was channeled by Jane Roberts (5). As soon he saw the book, he had goose bumps all over and he immediately knew that there was something here that he had to know more about.

But Esther did not want to hear about Seth. From she was a young child she had learnt to be both skeptical and afraid of anything that could be termed "supernatural", so she forbade Jerry to bring the Seth book into their bedroom. And when Jerry told their friends about Seth, Esther would quietly leave the room.

The more Jerry read of the Seth material, the more enthusiastic he became, because there he found answers to many of the questions that he had written down ever since he was six years old and to which he had been looking for answers in vain. Due to his enthusiasm Jerry couldn't help sneaking the thoughts of Seth into the conversations he had with Esther, and gradually she became increasingly open in as much as she realized that her skepticism mainly stemmed from old prejudice rather than experience from her own life. As she threw the antiquated beliefs over board, she became more and more enthusiastic about the Seth material, so much so that she eventually suggested to Jerry that they should go and visit Jane Roberts and her husband Robert Butts and thus "meet" Seth themselves.

But that meeting never came to be, because shortly afterwards Esther and Jerry were told that Jane Roberts had died. Through friends the couple then came into contact with another medium, who channeled a spiritual entity called Theo. Theo told Esther and Jerry, that they should try meditating, and that they themselves were channels. Their spiritual guide would present himself to them during meditation. Theo also said that when they, as a couple, had been selected to channel spiritual knowledge, it was because Esther had a strong ability to close out her own thoughts and calm her mind, and that Jerry through his lifelong quest for answers to the enigmas of life had attracted these answers.

Neither Jerry nor Esther knew how to meditate, and had always felt that it was something weird, which was not for normal people, but Theo had said: *"For 15 minutes every day you must sit in a quiet room wearing loose and comfortable clothes and focus on your breathing. When thoughts come, you must release them and bring your focus back to your breathing."* That sounded easy enough, so Esther and Jerry went home, put on their dressing gowns and sat down in their armchairs. However, they felt so uncomfortable about the situation that they put an étagère between them, so that they couldn't see each other.

Already during the first meditation, Esther felt that she went quite numb and that she practically floated in the air. During later meditations she felt that she was being breathed and that she was sitting in a wonderful, ecstatic energy. After nine months of meditation Abraham came through. It happened in the way that Esther's head moved on its own accord and she discovered that she wrote letters in the air with her nose. Jerry wrote the letters down and the message said: *"I am Abraham. I am your spiritual guide. I love you. I'm here to work with you"*.

Shortly afterwards Abraham began channeling knowledge to Esther by typing. She wrote so fast that Jerry was quite taken aback, because he couldn't follow the movements of her fingers on the keyboard with his eyes. Two months later Abraham spoke through Esther for the first time and on that occasion Jerry had a two-hour-long conversation with the group of spiritual beings that call themselves Abraham. That was in 1986.

That was how Jerry and Esther became mediators of the Abraham material. Today they have published a long series of books, CDs and DVDs, and they give several workshops every year all over the USA. They have recently been on an Oprah Winfrey show and in 2008 Esther Hicks appeared in Europe (London) for the first time to totally sold out houses (6).

Principal Features of Martinus' and Abraham's World Views

In order to understand the aim of this book, which is to point out how you can make the law of attraction work for you, it is first necessary to give a short outline of how both Martinus and Abraham view the world.

If you have a perception of life or a world view, which tells you that you are identical to your physical body, that you only live once, that death is the final end to life, that you live in a godless universe governed by chance and chaos, and that you yourself are just a passive pawn in the blind game of life, well, then you are in direct opposition to the world pictures of both Martinus and Abraham.

Both Martinus and Abraham agree that we are eternal beings and consequently we are far from identical to the body of flesh and blood with which we are used to identifying ourselves. Martinus goes as far as saying:

"When a living being thinks that he is identical with his physical body, he is subject to the biggest illusion that exists".

All of Martinus' work can be said to be one huge argument for the immortality of the living beings. A total death with cessation of consciousness and experience does absolutely not exist. What exists is just an exchange of bodies. Apart from our physical body we have a number of spiritual bodies, which are of an electrical nature. We shall have a much closer look at what happens when we "die" in part 2 of this book.

Also Abraham underlines again and again that we are immortal beings that right now have manifested our eternal "I" in a physical body. The "coming forth" into the physical body was a natural thing to do in view of the necessary experience of contrast that this "emergence into physical" would provide, but we are in no way identical to our physical body, which is "just" a temporary instrument for the "I". When we re-emerge into non-physical, or when we "die" (Abraham likes to use the word "croak" because it connotes disrespect – there is no death, so no respect is needed) we will immediately know that we are eternal beings, that we are extensions of "source energy", i.e. that we are part of the cosmic energy source of the universe. And just as what we call death is not the end to our experience of life, what we call birth is not the beginning either. We have incarnated here on the physical plane innumerable times before now, and for each time we reincarnate, we develop towards becoming perfect and complete human beings. We are eternal beings whose existence cannot cease. Our consciousness will always exist, because it is part of the consciousness of the universe or the source.

Martinus often refers to "the source" as God or Godhead, whereas Abraham mostly uses the expression "source" or "all that is". But both agree that an intelligent, creative and governing principle exists in the universe and that we are all part of it. Martinus says that we are "quanta of God" or "sons of God", whereas Abraham calls us "extensions of source energy". So both agree that we are part of something that is much bigger than us, and that right now we are on a visit to the physical plane. At intervals we emerge from the spiritual plane onto the physical plane in order to experience the details of this plane of existence. We have been here innumerable times before and we'll come here again innumerable times, because we are, as already mentioned, eternal beings that reincarnate again and again in physical matter in order to experience contrast.

The nature of the physical plane is such that it manifests in details that form a stark contrast to the nature of the spiritual plane. The physical plane is denser, heavier and darker than the spiritual plane, and on the physical plane it is possible to experience pain. The existence of the physical plane is of paramount importance because of the possibilities it offers to experience contrast, and without contrast, no experience of life. The experience of contrast is absolutely fundamental for the maintenance of our eternal ability to perceive, so for that reason the physical universe exists as a place where we can experience contrast to the spiritual world.

Abraham underlines the importance of contrast again and again. At the start of a session of channeling there will usually be a reference to the importance of the experience of contrast. As soon as Abraham comes through "he" will often start with the question to the audience: *"Are you enjoying your experience of contrast?"* "He" then usually goes on to say how important it is to experience this contrast and how much we wanted the experience of contrast before we reincarnated. The experience of contrast is so fundamental to our eternal ability to perceive that its importance cannot be exaggerated.

Furthermore both Martinus and Abraham underline repeatedly that life abounds on innumerable planets, indeed that there is life everywhere in the universe, which is an exorbitantly huge living being. In this living being of immensely gigantic dimensions life is teeming everywhere, so there are living beings like us on innumerable other planets. And not only that, but the planets themselves are living beings, so that also goes for our planet The Earth.

The Earth is a living being, and we are part of its microcosm and are cells in its body. As a living being The Earth has control of its body, and it regulates both the climate, the oxygen – and carbon dioxide content of the air, the salinity of the seas and the holes in the ozone layer. Consequently there is no reason to worry about climate change, because the climate is decided solely by the "I" of the Earth in cooperation with the Sun. With respect to the climate we are at the mercy of forces that are way beyond our control, and worrying about something that we cannot control is not the best choice of thoughts. We shall have a much more detailed look at this in part two.

The size of the population of both humans and animals is also under the control of the "I" of the earth being. The number of humans and different species of animals that inhabit The Earth is attended to from a much wider perspective, which means that it is controlled by metaphysical forces and it is not something that we humans have any major influence on. If the climatic conditions change, so that specific species no longer thrive here (for instance polar bears), then it isn't something that there is any reason to worry about because these animals will, through the law of attraction, in their next incarnation be attracted to planets, where the living conditions are better for their specific demands of habitat. Nobody is lost and nobody is "extinct". We just have to see things in a larger perspective.

Both Martinus and Abraham underline again and again that everything here on Earth is just as it should be. *"Everything is very good"* says Martinus – things are exactly as they should be considering the level of development that the Earth and we have reached. Everything is under control by forces that are much bigger and stronger than us. Also Abraham points out that the Earth is a wonderful and beautiful place to be, where conditions are ideal for the experience of contrast. When Jerry Hicks once mentioned to Abraham that the Earth *"was in a mess"* Abraham said angrily: *"The Earth is NOT in a mess"*. Actually Abraham goes as far as saying that life on Planet Earth has never been better and that it will get even better. Here on the Earth everything is under control and none of us micro beings has any reason at all to worry about the state of the planet, because it lies way beyond what we have control over. One can, in fact, compare all our talk about global warming with the possible worry of a handful of fleas that their host dog has a slight rise in temperature.

Abraham also underlines that we are here on the physical plane right now because we, before we incarnated here, had a strong yearning to get down here to experience and create. We are here to let our creative ability blossom, to experience contrast and well being. Our most important aim is to feel joy in the process, and our only criterion of success is, according to Abraham, the amount of joy we feel while we are here. We are not here to fix anything or to carry out anything specific. Abraham does not measure success in money, position or power, but solely in how much joy and pleasure we get from our sojourn on the physical plane.

Also Martinus points out that we are here according to our own wishes, and that the experience of life is its most fundamental meaning. Seen in the really large perspective the meaning of life is to experience it. Because we are part of the gigantic being we can call God, our experience of contrast is of fundamental importance to God's experience of life, as "he" experiences life within, via us, "his" micro beings. As God does not have a macro cosmos (a surrounding world that is bigger) or a meso cosmos (a world outside himself of similar size) "he" has to experience life within, through his micro cosmos. For that reason the experience of life is of fundamental importance, not only for the renewal of our own consciousness, but also for God's.

Why Martinus and Abraham together with respect to the law of attraction?

Now, somebody might ask why the Martinus and Abraham materials should be used together. Why not just let the two stand alone? When I have chosen to compare the two sets of material, it is because there is great value in letting them supplement each other. Held together the two sets of material support each other and thus they become a strong argument, not only for the workings of the law of attraction, but also for the immortality of the living beings, reincarnation and the existence of the spiritual world. The two different sources confirm each other – they basically agree.

Martinus is the theorist, the master, the cosmologist, who has the whole world picture. The Abraham material is not as comprehensive and extensive as that of Martinus, as it mostly deals with the law of attraction and other laws that have relation to this law. But then Abraham has lots of what the Martinus material hasn't: practical advice. What to do and how to do it. How do I bring my life to where I want it to be? How do I get happy? The Abraham material is a cornucopia of good advice.

Martinus is the theoretic and Abraham is the practician. The two agree that the law of attraction is the most powerful natural law of the universe. Indeed, even gravity is a result of the law of attraction and repulsion. We'll come back to that in part two of the book.

The law of attraction and repulsion is active all the time, even if we don't realize it. The law is not only active in nature and in everything that lies outside us, no – it is active in our own lives around the clock. And because it is active in our own lives around the clock, it is of great value to know the law and its workings. As long as we don't know the importance of the law in our own life and fate, we have no idea how to make it work for us. As long as we are ignorant about the workings of the law in our own lives, we grope around in the dark and may unknowingly create circumstances that are undesirable. Because the law of attraction is so important, we shall see how we can make it a co-worker instead of an opponent.

But first we shall have a look at what Martinus and Abraham have to say about thoughts, because it is with our thoughts that we attract. Our thoughts and feelings are of an electrical nature and with the quality of our thought climate we attract people, circumstances and events in our lives. But what are thoughts? Does it at all matter what we think? Can we decide what we think? We'll look at that important aspect in the next chapter.

4. What are thoughts?

Thoughts are electrical

As already mentioned thoughts are "something". This "something" is of an electrical nature, and it is precisely the electrical nature of thoughts that makes them measurable. When we can measure thought activity, it is the electrical current of the thoughts that we can measure. One can say that thoughts have a double nature: they contain information and at the same time they contain electricity or force. Force and information are two inseparable aspects of thoughts.

When thoughts are electrical, it consequently means that there is both force and magnetism in thoughts. It is this magnetism we sense when we say that a certain person has radiation. Radiation is not something we can actually see, but we often sense that a certain person has "something" – it can be a positive, negative, happy, moody, helpful, calm, kind, nervous etc. radiation. This radiation mainly stems from the nature of that person's being and thoughts, and it is the force or magnetism of the thoughts that determines that we can pick up another person's radiation.

Because thoughts are small power sources they are a factor, not only in what we radiate, but in the whole magnetism of the organism. For that reason it is of major importance what type of thoughts we think. With our thoughts we magnetize the organism – positively or negatively.

Our thoughts form an electrical field which flows through the organism, but which also transgresses the limits of the organism and "sits" like a bubble around the physical body. It is this bubble or radiation, which is often referred to as our aura. The aura is the electrical field around the body, whose quality or vibration is mainly determined by our thoughts and their quality. Happy, positive thoughts create a different vibration than unhappy, negative thoughts. With the quality of our thoughts we magnetize our organism.

Some people can see auras, but today it is also possible to visualize the aura through the use of a technique developed by the Russian scientist Semyon D. Kirlian.

Aura visualized through the Kirlian technique

Consciousness

Today there is a tendency to view consciousness as a result of the functioning of the physical body – indeed, consciousness is viewed as something which just arises from the chemical reactions of the body. But nothing could be more incorrect. Our consciousness consists of electromagnetic radiation (ray-formed matter), and it is this type of matter, that enlivens the body on the strength of its electrical nature.

"...there is an exceedingly important aspect of the appearance of the living being that consists of ray-formed matter, indeed this aspect is so important that it in reality predominates the whole being. It constitutes its complete consciousness function, i.e. everything that goes through the senses in the shape of thoughts and experiences, be it happiness and sorrow, primitivism and intellectuality, in short every aspect of the "consciousness" of the living being. But consciousness is again the same as the sensation of being alive. Without consciousness, no experience and consequently no life. Consciousness and life are identical. Through this it has become a fact to us that the living being consists of two big combinations of matter, a physical and a ray-formed. The physical consists solely of subordinate organs that are exploited by the ray-formed". (Martinus:"Through Death", Kosmos 5, 2005).

The totality of our being consists of two types of matter: The physical matter and the ray-formed matter. The physical body is "just" an instrument for the consciousness or the ray-formed matter. The physical body can be likened to a lamp. A lamp is just a combination of various physical parts, it is an instrument whose mission it is to light up a room. The lighting up of the room only happens when the ray-formed matter or the electricity is added. Only when electricity is added does the lamp function. In the same way as the lamp is useless without the electricity, the physical body is equally useless without the electricity pertaining to the consciousness forces or "I". Both the lamp and the physical body are subordinate instruments that only function when the ray-formed matter is added.

This means that the ray-formed matter is the primary force in the body: it is the carrier of our "I" or self, it holds our consciousness and our entire thought sphere. It carries force and information at the same time. Our whole consciousness is electrical in its nature. Because electricity contains force, our consciousness constitutes our life force. Consciousness and life are identical. With its life force the consciousness enlivens the physical body, which is an instrument for the "I". The physical body is, via its ingenious chemical / physical construction, a unique instrument used by the consciousness or "I" for its experience of the physical world. Without the physical world no experience of contrast could take place, and without the experience of contrast, no renewal of consciousness. In the perspective of eternity the experience of contrast is of incontestable importance.

Our complete spiritual body or aura constitutes our consciousness. The consciousness consists of the thoughts we are thinking here and now, and the experiences we remember, but it also holds a whole series of other "ingredients", which mainly are results of experiences reaped in former incarnations and "stored" in our spiritual body. Thus our consciousness encompasses our whole mentality, talents and abilities, character traits, patterns of reaction, habits and tendencies, wishes and will, ability to believe, knowledge, feelings, moral, ability to love, level of intelligence, our fears and phobias, indeed, our whole personality and sense of self. All of these aspects of consciousness manifest themselves as thoughts and feelings, and as they are electrical in their nature, they are electromagnetic rays and waves on specific wavelengths. The totality of our consciousness constitutes an electrical field, and this field operates on a specific wavelength. Because no two sets of consciousness hold identical thoughts, talents, character traits etc. there will be individual differences between the wavelengths of different consciousnesses.

The seat of consciousness is not the brain, but the spiritual body or aura – the electrical field that both surrounds and penetrates the body. The brain can be likened to an antenna, where the thought energies embedded in the field can enter the day-conscious area via the membrane of the brain. The brain is not the seat of consciousness and thoughts do not arise in the brain – they are "caught" by the antenna of the brain in agreement with the wishes of the "I". According to the will of the "I" the thoughts can then be directed to the nervous system and on to any part of the body. If the thought contains an order to a muscle group to make the body sit, stand or walk, the muscles will act accordingly. The body is an obedient subject for the electrical forces of the "I".

The Enormous Power of Thought

There is enormous power in our thoughts – indeed with our thoughts we create both our level of health and our fate. We create our own reality with our thoughts. If we go around believing that it doesn't matter what we think and that it is of no importance which thoughts we allow to dominate our mentality, we are the victims of a huge illusion. Our thoughts are the most important factor in our lives. We create our fate by maintaining a mental picture in our thoughts of how we want our lives to unfold. When we can see it in our mind's eye, it will happen sooner or later (more about this in chapter 6). And we create our state of health by thinking health and by seeing ourselves as healthy, sane, fit and fully functional all through life.

"So, an illness has two primary stages. First it has a stage, which we could call the stage of the "cause". From this stage it develops into the stage of the "effect", which means the stage of "pain and inconvenience". The stage of cause does not exist on the physical plane; it only exists in the psyche or mental area of the individual. It is here that all illnesses have their first or original source, just as all kinds of absolute wellbeing also have their inner source here." (Martinus: "Sickness and Cure", Kosmos 5, 1997).

Both illness and wellbeing have their source in the psyche. Health and illness arise on the thought plane first. Those, who can see auras, can often see the primary stages of sickness in the shape of grey "lumps" in the aura. These "lumps" can sometimes be treated through healing before they get a physical expression, i.e. before the illness manifests in the physical body. It is also possible to cleanse one's aura by changing one's way of thinking, by thinking healthy and positive thoughts. But if the "lumps" remain untreated and are allowed "to settle" they will result in an illness in the physical body. Illness always arises on the thought plane first, as an "unfortunate" vibration in the aura, which can become predominant if it isn't neutralized through a change in the vibration. And a vibration can only be changed by changing one's way of thinking.

If you allow your thoughts to be dominated by the idea of a specific illness or the idea that you will surely inherit a specific illness from your parents, well, then that specific illness will sooner or later manifest in your body unless you change your way of thinking. If you, instead of focusing on an illness, focus on your total health and see yourself jumping around in the surroundings of your choice, happy as a mountain goat and free as a bird, well, then you magnetize your organism positively, your vibration becomes high and enhancing for health, and illness will be a thing of the past.

But are thoughts really so important? Let us have a look at what Martinus and Abraham say about the importance of thoughts.

With Our Thoughts We Create Our State of Health

Abraham says that there is a direct correlation between what you are thinking about and what is actually coming into your experience. Nothing merely shows up in your experience. You attract it – all of it. No exceptions. You are creating your own reality with the predominant thoughts in your mind. If those thoughts are concentrated on illness, then you will inevitably attract that illness.

Martinus is in total agreement and says that our way of thinking constitutes the most important creative factor in the organism of the individual.

"What, then, is thinking since it plays such an important role in the life of the individual? Thinking is a concentrated release of "overphysical" forces through the brain and nervous system of the individual. According to "Livets Bog" "over-physical" forces are the same as higher electrical waves or vibrations. The reception and emission of these waves through the organism are perceived as "thoughts". Again, this perception is the same as the experience of life. When an individual thinks, it means that a current of electrical waves goes through its brain and nervous system. The brain and nervous system can in this connection be viewed as a "radio receiver" of an extremely fine construction and the electrical current is, in comparison to ordinary radio waves, extremely microscopic. While this current is inwardly perceived as thought, as experience of life, it is outwardly manifested as "magnetism", which again, in this case, is the same as what we call "life force".

As the thoughts are thus the same as fine electrical waves that flow through the organism, all thinking will be identical to some kind of "electrification" of the organism, which again in this case means the same as an overphysical filling up of force. This "electrification" or filling up of force is released directly into the blood. Thus the thinking becomes the highest foundation for the creation of the blood, <u>and its quality totally depends on the nature and quality of the thinking.</u> As the blood again constitutes the very foundation for the creation, maintenance and wellbeing of the organism itself, <u>the thinking thus becomes the highest manifestation factor of life.</u>- What a _being thinks, it becomes_. *If it has sickly and abnormous thoughts, its organism will be sickly or abnormously magnetized and to the same degree it must manifest as unhealthy and weak. With light, healthy and normal thoughts it will inevitably manifest as an expression of the highest normal wellbeing."* (Martinus: "On Funerals", chapter 43, my underlining added).

What Martinus reveals in this quotation about the importance of thinking is of great consequence. Because thoughts are of an electrical nature, are fine, electrical waves and consequently magnetic, they are identical to the life force of the individual. A thought is a small source of power, a small "topping up" of force of the organism. It is quite simply so that we electrify our organism with our thoughts, and this electrification is released directly into the blood. The quality of the blood depends on the quality and nature of the thinking. And as the blood circulates into every nook and cranny of the body, there will not be a single cell that isn't affected by the quality and magnetization of the blood. For that reason it is of paramount importance which thoughts we think, because the quality of the thinking affects the organism and its state of health immediately. What you think, you become. Happy and positive thoughts affect the organism positively and lead to good health, while discontent, bitter and negative thoughts affect the organism negatively and lead to lack of health and all sorts of illnesses.

Let's have a look at what Martinus says about the origin of certain illnesses in the following quotation:

"It is dangerous to have evil thoughts or be angry and bitter and bother other people, and it is not just an external danger, but also an internal danger, because the individual types of thoughts are life forces that affect specific organs within us. We can have thoughts that work directly on the heart and create a heart condition. This may come without our realizing it, if we have hated for years and have been constantly bitter and get angry at the slightest thing. We can have thoughts that work on the stomach and generate ulcers, other thoughts work on the brain and can finally lead to insanity, while others again can ruin the muscles, the skin etc." (Martinus: "God's Eyes", Kosmos 2, 2008).

The Placebo Effect

Now, this may not be anything new, as medical science has known for a long time that positive and happy people in general are healthier and more resistant to infections than negative and bitter people. It is a well-known fact that our thoughts are of importance to our health and healing, because the effect has been studied through the use of the so-called placebo medication.

Placebo medication can be a completely ineffective chalk tablet without any kind of active ingredient. But when the patient is administered with the chalk tablet and at the same time is told that the tablet will cure or alleviate some aliment, then it has been found that the desired effect did set in, irrespective of the fact that the tablet had no other effect than making the patient believe in the cure. But the belief in the positive effect was enough for it to alleviate and heal. Intensive investigations have been carried out over the last 50 years into the placebo effect through hundreds of experiments all over the world, and today it has been established that about 50 % of those, who were given placebo medication, experienced a marked improvement of their state of health. It has been found that placebo medication is effective against a whole series of illnesses such as: allergy, fever, colds, migraines, acne, asthma, warts, see sickness and other forms of nausea, ulcers, arthritis, diabetes, scleroses, Parkinson's disease, angina pectoris and cancer (7).

In Chinese medicine it has for centuries been a well-established fact that the healing effect of a certain medication depends on the doctor who prescribes it. If the medication is prescribed by an old, experienced doctor its effect is considerably higher than if it has been prescribed by a young and not so experienced doctor. The young doctor may be just as knowledgable as the old doctor in the particular disease, but it is the patient's perceived faith in the doctor's knowledge and experience that is decisive for the healing effect.

Examples of the Power of Thought in Sickness and Healing

There are many examples of how our thoughts can make us ill or well. Let us have a look at some of them.

When we moved to Spain we necessarily also left behind the Danish health system. If we wanted to be covered in the same way as we were in Denmark, we had to take out a private health insurance. But such an insurance was expensive, and we simply could not afford it. That meant that in the future we had to live without being insured against illness and accidents. So we said to each other: *"Well, then we just have to keep healthy. We "just" have to envisage ourselves as totally well and healthy at all times"*. It is the best thing we have ever done to our health. Today, 18 years later, we can truly say that we have had no kind of illness that needed treatment. We have been just as well and healthy as we then said we would be.

On the other hand we often see among our patients in the dental practice examples that confirm that those, who talk a lot about illness also suffer from a whole series of illnesses. In particular there was a couple that talked about illness all the time. Their thoughts were constantly occupied with all sorts of ailments from broken bones to skin cancer, osteoporosis, boils and infections, diabetes, renal problems, heart problems, liver problems etc. Not only did they talk about them, they suffered from all of them and their lives were one long commuting between home and hospital.

But then we also see patients that are in their 70s and that still run around in the mountains like mountain goats and never think about illness. They see themselves as well and fit, and they are. They go hiking in the Himalayas and in the Atlas Mountains, they walk across the Anatolian plain, on the Inca Trail up to Machu Picchu, they hike along Corfu, around Cyprus and the Azores, indeed the list of places they have hiked is longer than the list of cows subsidized by the EU. They do not subscribe to the thought that age means frailty and inactivity, but continue to see themselves in the physical shape they had in their 30s. And they have it – they are well, fully fit and totally healthy.

I have also seen an example of how our thoughts can kill us.

Before we moved to Spain, I was working as a teacher at a secondary school in Århus, Denmark. I had a colleague, who was obsessed with the thought that passive smoking could give her lung cancer. If somebody smoked in the staff room (it was before smoking was banned in the work place), she became very aggressive and demonstratively opened the windows and waved magazines and newspapers to get the smoke out. She complained in no uncertain terms and yelled at the smokers that passive smoking could kill us all. She was totally unrelaxed, indeed close to hysterical, to any kind of smoking and I'm sure that every time she was exposed to passive smoking, she unconsciously told her body, that now it was dying from lung cancer. However it may be, she was taken ill only a few months after being employed and after 3 months she died from lung cancer. She had never smoked herself, but still she died from lung cancer. It is likely that she, every time she came into contact with other people's tobacco smoke, unconsciously told her body that now it was dying from lung cancer. And so it happened. Her thoughts became her reality and became her fate, because the thoughts are the biggest factor in the health of our body. What we think, we become.

This example clearly illustrates the importance of knowing the far-reaching effects of our thoughts, because if we don't know it and think that it doesn't matter what we think, we can unknowingly attract unwanted states of health.

Another example is one where a shift in thoughts from worry to laughter cured a man from stomach cancer. This man had been diagnosed with inoperable cancer and had been told that he only had three months to live. He then decided that he would spend these last three months in the best manner he could think of, and as he loved funny movies and particularly funny cartoons, he decided to move into a hotel and spend the last months having fun. He bought and borrowed all the funny movies he could lay his hands on, and spent the days laughing and enjoying himself. When the three months has passed, he was expecting death to come, but he did not feel ill and decided to go back to hospital to see what his doctor said. The doctor examined him and found that there was no longer any trace of cancer. *"What cancer? Your cancer has disappeared!"* The heightened vibration and change of focus from illness to laughter had completely cured the man.

Is cancer infectious? Well, not in a traditional sense, but cases where it seems so are not unusual. We knew a young couple in their late 20s where the girl had been diagnosed with cancer of the uterus. This was a complete chock and the couple staked all their energy and focus on her healing. Her father was a medical doctor, so the girl underwent a long treatment of chemotherapy. Finally and after a long, hard treatment the cancer subsided, but then the young man was diagnosed with a very severe cancer. This is not because the cancer is infectious, but because the intense focusing on the cancer attracts the illness. If you think about cancer for many hours every day, well, then you will sooner or later manifest the illness yourself. You cannot focus on a serious illness for many hours every day and then at the same time attract health. It is against the natural laws. Whatever you focus on is what you attract.

A very well known example of the placebo effect is the case of Mr. Wright, who suffered from advanced cancer of the lymph nodes (8). Mr. Wright was a patient of Dr. Bruno Klopfner who has related the case. Mr. Wright had tumors the size of oranges on his neck, chest, abdomen, groin and armpits. His spleen and liver were enlarged, and from his chest two liters of milky liquid had to be drained every day. Mr. Wright could hardly breathe and had been given up by the medical staff. But Mr. Wright did not want to die; he still believed there was something that could cure him. He had heard about a promising new drug called Krebiozen, and he begged Dr. Klopfner to try it on him. Dr. Klopfner was reluctant to do so, because the medical team wanted to test the drug on patients that had a three to six months life expectancy and Mr. Wright was only expected to live a few days. But because Mr. Wright insisted, Dr. Klopfner agreed to give him an injection of Krebiozen on Friday, expecting him to be dead when he came back to the hospital on Monday.

To Dr. Klopfner's great surprise, on the Monday he found Mr. Wright out of bed and walking around. He checked on the other patients who had been injected with the drug, but they showed no sign of improvement. Only Mr. Wright showed a fantastic improvement. The tumors had melted like snowballs on a hot stove and were half the size they were three days ago. This was a much faster decrease in size than even the strongest chemotherapy could have accomplished. Dr. Klopfner continued with the injections of the drug, and after ten days Mr. Wright left the hospital, cancer free. In ten days this terminal patient had been completely cured of his cancer and was well enough to fly his own plane at 12.000 feet with no discomfort.

Mr. Wright remained well for two months, but then articles began to appear in the press about the ineffectiveness of Krebiozen. The drug did not seem to work. This worried Mr. Wright, who now felt that he was losing his only hope. He went into remission and was hospitalized again.

Dr. Klopfner then decided to try an experiment with Mr. Wright. He told Mr. Wright that Krebiozen really was as promising as had been said, but that the first deliveries were a bit weak. He told him that the hospital would receive a new, doubly effective supply of the drug on the following day, and that he would administer this drug to him. Now Mr. Wright regained his optimism and enthusiastically awaited his new treatment. Dr. Klopfner now injected Mr. Wright with a plain saline solution, pretending it was the doubly effective new version of Krebiozen.

Again the results were dramatic, even more impressive than the first time. The tumors disappeared as the daily injections of the saline solution continued. Mr. Wright left the hospital, he flew again, he was the epitome of good health.

He was symptom free for two months, but then the American Medical Association announced that a nationwide study of Krebiozen had found the drug worthless in the treatment of cancer.

A few days after this announcement, Mr. Wright was hospitalized again. He no longer had anything to pin his hopes on and he died within two days.

This fantastic story clearly shows that our thoughts can heal us. As long as Mr. Wright believed in the effects of the medication, it worked and then it didn't matter if it *was* the drug Krebiozen or just a saline solution. The effect was the same, and as long as Mr. Wright believed that he could be healed, he was healed. The example also shows that healing can be obtained in a very, very short time. Abraham says that healing is only a thought away. As soon as you are able to think healing, fear free and hopeful thoughts, wellness follows step by step.

Thoughts Are Small Sources of Power

That there actually IS power in thoughts can be substantiated via the immediate effects that certain thoughts and feelings have on the organism. We all know that a certain thought can make us blush, can make the heart beat faster and make perspiration appear on the forehead. It is the thought of this or that that causes the reaction and nothing else. If there was no force or power in thoughts, such a reaction could not take place. Martinus expresses it like this:

"That the thought is actually a force that binds or keeps the organism in a certain state is, among other things, visible in the facial expressions of the individual. Alone the fact that these can be different shows that behind the face there is a force that is decisive for the gestures of the facial muscles. A face can express anger and hatred one moment and mildness and love another moment. That there is anger behind thoughts of anger and love behind thoughts of love is a fact to every normal person. But if these thoughts were not a force, an energy, they would not be able to influence anything, and consequently they could have no influence on the facial muscles. Then they would not, as it is now sometimes the case, be able to make the blood "flush to the cheeks", make the heart beat faster, make the individual blush or pale. Any face would be stiff as that of a statue, just as it would be impossible to move arms and legs." (Martinus: "On Funerals", chapter 44).

Our thoughts are electrical and consequently they contain force. It is this force which immediately affects our facial muscles, so that it is, in many cases, possible to "read" what a person thinks. When we have happy thoughts, these are reflected in the face and so are angry and hateful thoughts. The force in the thoughts not only affects the facial muscles directly, but all our muscles, so that we can move our limbs. The force of the thought affects the muscles directly, so that they immediately carry out the task that the thought decrees. The moment we think that now I want to raise my right arm, the arm is already raised. It means that our thoughts are subject to our will.

"As the supreme ruler and master of this mesocosmic electricity or life force, which has been born by the thought impulses, your "I" or highest Self exists". (Martinus: "Answer to a letter from a sick person", Kosmos 5, 2007).

It is our "I" or higher self that is the supreme ruler of our thought impulses and the force inherent in them. It is in other words the "I" that rules supreme in our organism. This again means that we can decide what we want to think about and consequently we can influence our state of health.

But not only that: with our thoughts we also shape the circumstances of our life. We attract the people, who become our friends and lovers, indeed, we attract what becomes our fate. We shall look at how we do that in the next chapter.

5. The Law of Attraction and Repulsion

In order to understand how we can attract circumstances, our state of health, our friends, our lovers, and our fate it is a prerequisite to understand that everything is vibration. A specific vibration is an expression of the wavelength and frequency that a specific type of matter emits. All matter is vibration; all types of matter have a specific vibration, which is different from the vibration of other types of matter. But also all living beings have a specific vibration and this vibration is, to a large extent, defined by the thoughts and feelings of the being.

Everything Is Vibration

"They [the types of matter] are each and every one of them an expression of a specific type of energy or vibration. Gold, silver, cobber and iron or all metals thus have their own specific vibration, just as flesh, blood, juices, acids, sugar, salt, fruits, roots, kernels, leaves, stalks etc., etc. have…All these realities express different strong or weak vibrations, which together necessarily must represent a specific standard of force, which again means a specific measuring unit for energy or vibration ". (Martinus: "The Ideal Food", chapter 21, booklet 5).

"Again the vibrations represent an endless world of variations, which appear to the senses as colors, sounds, beams, bodies, in short as everything known to us as "created things". (Martinus: "The Ideal Food", chapter 13).

Our own bodies have vibration, and when we can hear, see, sense, taste and smell, it is because the different types of matter have different vibrations, which impress our senses differently. Also the different colors and taste impressions are "only" expressions of waves that vibrate on different wavelengths. A red color has a vibration that is different from the vibration of a blue color, and salt has a vibration that is different from that of sugar. Because these two different expressions of vibration affect our taste buds differently, we are able to distinguish between them and we say that they taste salt and sweet respectively.

A vibration is an expression of a specific "entangled" combination of energy, i.e. an expression of energy in a specific "shape". This shape is expressed via the wavelength and frequency of the vibration.

"But an electric amount of energy, which has a specific limitation, can only be expressed as a "wavelength". But a "wavelength" can again only be directed by attraction and repulsion". (Martinus: "The Ideal Food", chapter 13).

There is only one way to direct wavelengths, and that is by attraction and repulsion. We have known for more than 100 years that wavelengths can be directed through attraction and repulsion. It is quite simply a natural law that decrees that similar wavelengths attract each other and that dissimilar wavelengths repel each other. Vibration and wavelength and the mutual attraction of similar wavelengths are simply the foundation of the functioning of the universe. We live in a universe whose basic way of functioning is determined by attraction and repulsion.

Macro- , Meso-, and Microcosmic Attraction

The strength or power of the attraction is defined by the size of the thing vibrating or attracting. For that reason we can talk about macrocosmic attraction, i.e. mutual attraction between celestial bodies, mesocosmic attraction, i.e. attraction between things or bodies in our surroundings, and microcosmic attraction, i.e. attraction between cells, molecules, particles, atoms etc. Naturally the attraction of large things will be stronger than that of smaller things, but even the smallest particle has some kind of attraction. We shall have a look at macrocosmic attraction in the second part of the book.

Thoughts and Will

With our thoughts we emit a specific vibration, and this vibration will attract identical vibrations or vibrations on the same wavelength as those we are thinking about. We can say that the thought that is predominant right now in our consciousness is our point of attraction. It is with the predominant thought that we attract. It works like this because our thoughts function like a kind of magnet and with our thoughts we attract what we are thinking about. That is simply how things work due to the attraction that identical wavelengths have on each other. We are talking about a well-known and well-defined natural law that is active all the time.

Abraham puts it like this: *What I'm thinking and what I'm feeling in response to what I'm thinking and what manifests is always a vibrational match. Every time. No exception.*

So, with our thoughts we attract what we are thinking about. And our thoughts are subject to our will. That means that we can decide, what we want to think. That again means that the spiritual attraction we emit to our surroundings is subject to our will. The importance of this realization cannot be exaggerated, because it means that we ourselves can decide which events, states of health, objects and people we attract. Because we can choose what we want to think about, we can choose what we want to attract into our lives.

When we change our thoughts with our will, for instance from negative to positive, then we change the vibration of our thoughts. Negative and positive thoughts have dissimilar vibrations. When we change the vibration of a thought we also change the wavelength that the thought operates on. And because similar wavelengths attract each other, then we will, once we let go of the negative thoughts and replace them with positive, attract positive wavelengths.

The prerequisite for us to begin attracting what we want is that we know about the workings of the law of attraction and that we **consciously** begin to attract the things and people we want to have in our lives. It is so that nobody can make the best of a law whose existence they are ignorant about. But when a universal law exists, which furthermore is the most important law, indeed the whole principle on which the functioning of the universe is based, well, then it is quite disadvantageous to be ignorant about the functioning of the law. Because when you are ignorant about the functioning of the law and believe that your fate is completely governed by chance, well, then you can unknowingly create circumstances in your life that are completely unwanted. You can for instance create illness, poverty, childlessness, loneliness, misery and a whole range of other unwanted circumstances *just because you are ignorant about the law of attraction and its importance in your life.*

Now somebody might claim that we don't decide our thoughts ourselves, because they experience how the thoughts are milling around in their heads without them having control of what they are thinking. But we can always consciously choose our thoughts. If you experience that you don't have any control over your thoughts, then it is because you haven't practiced controlling what you want to think. You **can** choose your thoughts yourself and as always you get better at it the more you practice.

Many people experience that they walk around thinking about things they don't want to happen. They are pessimists; they worry all the time about this and that and can, for instance, be thinking: now that I'm going away on holiday, my house is sure to be burgled. Their thoughts keep milling around this burglary, and thus they have set energies in motion that will make the burglary happen. But that is not what they wanted. But even if they know that it is an inappropriate thought, they cannot let it go.

How do you get rid of unwanted thoughts? Do you just shout "no" and "go away" to the thought to make it disappear? No, that is not how things work, because even if you shout "no" to the thought, then it is still a predominant thought in your consciousness. And when the thought is predominant in your consciousness, then it is your point of attraction. If you want to change your point of attraction, then you must change your thought.

This is what Abraham says: "*Without exception, that which you give thought to is that which you begin to invite into your experience. When you think a little thought about what you want, through The Law of Attraction, that thought grows larger and larger and more and more powerful. When you think a thought about something you do not want, the Law of Attraction draws onto it, and it grows larger and larger, also. And so, the larger the thought grows, the more power it draws onto it, and the more certain you are to receive the experience. When you see something you would like to experience and you say, "Yes, I would like to have that," through your attention to it you invite it into your experience. However, when you see something that you do not want to experience and you shout, "No, no, I do not want that!" through your attention to it you invite that into your experience. In this attraction-based Universe, there is no such thing as exclusion. Your attention to it includes it in your vibration, and if you hold it in your attention or awareness long enough, the Law of Attraction will bring it into your experience, for there is no such thing as "No".* (Esther and Jerry Hicks: "The Law of Attraction", page 31).

We shall look at how to deactivate unwanted thoughts in a later chapter.

"Birds of a Feather Flock Together"

There is a lot of wisdom in many of the old sayings and in both Danish and English we have examples of expressions that reflect the law of attraction. In Danish we say "krage søger mage" (the crow seeks its mate) and "lige børn leger bedst" (children of equal means are the best playmates), and in English we know the expression "birds of a feather flock together" and "that, which is like onto itself, is drawn". These sayings express that individuals with similar dispositions and inclinations tend to find each other.

Let us have a look at what Martinus says about the importance of the law of attraction and repulsion.

"*Through the law of attraction and repulsion the whole of the divine administration and method of creation is organized. It is this law that causes dogs to have puppies, cats to give birth to kittens and human beings to be born to other human beings. But it is not only in the area of births that this law is decisive. It is also this law that lies behind the old reality of "krage søger mage", and "lige børn leger bedst". Thus it determines that related species seek related species. It also follows that the same law of life causes people at the same level of development to mainly seek out each others' company, become affiliates of the same parties, political as well as religious...This again means that people who tend to have the same moral views, the same mentality and behavior become more and more concentrated in the same groups.*" (Martinus: Collection of Articles 1, "Doomsday" 12.8).

Martinus confirms that it is no unimportant law that we are looking at, but rather a law through which the whole of the divine administration and method of creation is organized. The law of attraction is simply the corner stone in the whole functioning of the universe. Our universe has been created in the way that the mutual attraction of identical wavelengths is the main factor in the functioning and reactions of both physical and spiritual types of matter.

It is the law of attraction that determines which groups we belong to, who we get together with, who we feel sympathy for, who we fall in love with etc. And it is also the law of attraction that determines which parents we are born to. It is no chance occurrence who becomes our parents in a specific incarnation. Through the law of attraction we will, in our spiritual body from the spiritual plane, be attracted to precisely the lovemaking couple, whose combined wavelength is similar to ours. That means that we will be born to parents who resemble us with respect to talents, tendencies, race and species. We shall have a closer look at this interesting aspect in part two.

Our Emotional Guidance System

When we can choose our thoughts, it is important that we become good at choosing the most appropriate thoughts – thoughts that bring health and happiness. To help us distinguish between what is a good and appropriate thought and what is a bad and inappropriate thought we have a fantastic built in measuring instrument that never errs: our emotional guidance system. The emotion we register in connection with a specific thought will immediately pass its judgment. The emotion we register in connection with any thought will immediately and with great accuracy tell us if it is something that we can go on thinking and consequently attract, or if it is something that we should keep away from and consequently immediately stop attracting.

This is what Abraham says: *"If you focus upon whatever you want, you will attract whatever you want. If you focus upon the lack of whatever you want, you will attract more of the lack. (Every subject is really two subjects: what you want and the lack, or absence, of what you want.) If you are paying attention to what you are feeling, you will always know whether you are focused upon what you want or upon the lack of it – for when you are thinking of what you want, you are feeling good, and when you are thinking of the lack of what you want, you are feeling bad."* (Esther and Jerry Hicks: "The Law of Attraction", page 86).

The thought of illness will make most people feel uncomfortable and thus their emotional guidance system has told them that it is a thought to avoid. The thought about a date with one's lover will make most people feel happy, and again the emotional guidance system has spoken – it is OK to think about it and thus attract the circumstances of the date.

It is of great importance that we learn to "listen" to or "read" our emotional guidance system, because there we have free and infallible guidance from our higher self about what to think, do and cause.

"But what then is attraction and repulsion in this connection? Well, it is, in this case as in all other vicissitudes of life of "electrical" nature. As attraction and repulsion is the same as the feeling of sympathy and antipathy respectively towards something in the individual's surroundings and daily life, the afore mentioned realities will in effect be identical to a higher form of a real "magnetic" function between the "self" and the object of the sympathy or antipathy. This "magnetic" function or attraction and repulsion is, just like everything else in life, subject to specific laws." (Martinus: "About my Cosmic Analysis", chapter 11, booklet 12: "The Road to Initiation").

What Martinus says here is that we mainly have two different ways of perceiving our surroundings: we either feel sympathy or we feel antipathy. Whether we feel sympathy or antipathy is again a result of our own vibrational state. We will feel sympathy towards that which vibrates on a wavelength similar to our own mental or spiritual forces, and we will feel antipathy towards that which vibrates on a wavelength that is far from our own vibration. We are simply talking about a factual magnetic attraction or repulsion. We are attracted to those with whom we are on wavelength and we are repelled by those with whom we are not on wavelength. And it is in reality this "mechanism" that makes like-minded people "find" each other, and this is valid whether we are talking about political parties, religious societies, ornithologists, philatelists, motorcycle enthusiasts, golf players or wine enthusiasts.

Also Abraham points out that our emotional guidance system is our best auxiliary tool in connection with our choice of an object of attraction. Abraham agrees with Martinus that there are only two feelings in connection with an immediate reaction: antipathy or sympathy. Or said in a simpler way: it either feels good or it feels bad. Even if our physical body isn't equipped with a visible measuring instrument on which we can read what we are attracting, then our emotional guidance system is just as accurate an instrument as a thermometer on which we can read the quality of our thought and the appropriateness of our point of attraction.

This "mechanism", that lets us feel sympathy for certain aspects of life and for certain people, and antipathy for other aspects and other people, is a fantastic built-in compass that we have, and which we really should learn to pay attention to. Because when we learn to "listen" to our emotional guidance system in every situation and in connection with every thought, then we have the best compass in the world indicating where to go and what to avoid. Stop and listen to what you feel! If it feels good, it is an OK thought to have and an

OK situation to be in, but if it feels bad or wrong, then choose another thought or stay away from the situation. Change course and chose another destination.

Let us look at an example: You are a peace loving person and now you are walking along the street. About 100 meters further along you see a group of "Hell's Angels" hanging out. Your immediate reaction is repulsion or antipathy, and if you are listening to your emotion, it will tell you to walk down a side street or onto the other pavement in order not to get into trouble. However, if you are a "Hell's Angel" yourself, you will feel sympathy for the group and walk right up to it and say hello to the members. It is the law of attraction and repulsion in action.

Your emotions are also a super barometer for which thoughts are good and which thoughts are bad for you to nourish. If you think about a sunny tropical island with white sandy beaches and swaying palm trees, you will probably feel sympathy and that means that it is an OK thought to feed to your consciousness. But if you are thinking that now you'll soon get a cancerous growth in your stomach, well, then it is highly likely that you'll feel antipathy at the thought. When the antipathy floods your being, then it is an indicator that this is not a good thought to feed your consciousness with. Your emotional guidance system has passed its verdict and it tells you that this is something to steer clear of. This is simply a thought to avoid, because if you don't avoid it, then it will attract what you are thinking about. That is how the law of attraction works: you attract what you think about. Frequent and repeated thoughts about this cancerous growth will attract it. There is nothing mysterious about that, because that is how the law of attraction works, and it ALWAYS works, because it *is a natural law.* If you think about a specific illness again and again, you will attract it – you cannot fail, because this is dictated by the strongest law of the universe.

Attraction of Unwanted Circumstances

Abraham points out that we create our life and our reality through what we attract with our thoughts. But many people cannot accept this, because they have unwanted circumstances in their lives, be it illness, poverty, loneliness etc, which they do not think they have created themselves. To this Abraham says that it is 100% certain that they have created them, because otherwise they could not have manifested in their lives. But Abraham also says that it is obvious that they have not created the unwanted circumstances consciously and on purpose.

This is how Abraham puts it: *"People often explain, in the midst of unwanted things occurring in their experience, that they are certain **they** did not create such a thing. "I wouldn't have done this unwanted thing to myself!" they* *explain. And while we know that you did not deliberately bring this unwanted thing into your experience, we must still explain that only **you** could have caused it, for no one else has the power to attract what comes to you but you".* (Esther and Jerry Hicks: "The Law of Attraction", page 30).

It is obvious that nobody creates unwanted circumstances for themselves on purpose. All the same, when it happens again and again that you create something unwanted, there are, according to Abraham, mainly two reasons for this. The first reason is that you don't know the law of attraction and consequently are ignorant about the fact that you attract what you think about. This lack of knowledge about the law of attraction can, of course, mean that you have dwelt on sad thoughts, worry, illness, and pessimism without knowing that you have thus been attracting these circumstances. Unknowingly and without wanting to, you have attracted what is a vibrational match to the predominant pessimistic thoughts in your consciousness.

The other reason is that we are not happy enough. An unhappy basic state of mind attracts unhappiness. We can have set our point of vibration too low – so low and with so little "joi de vivre" that what we attract are unwanted circumstances that are on vibrational wavelength with our own, low, unhappy vibration. When it is at all possible to set our point of vibration on "low" and "unhappy", it is because we are not sufficiently aware of our emotional guidance system. Somewhere along the way we have accepted that it is OK / normal / acceptable that we are not well / content / happy. In other words we have accepted to feel other than happy. And when it is at all possible to accept such an unhappy state of mind, it is because we have stopped listening to our emotional guidance system.

It is the job of the emotional guidance system to tell us that we are now "below zero" and that it would be appropriate to move up the emotional scale towards content, harmonious, happy, grateful etc. But many people have become really good at ignoring this guidance. They don't care that they feel "down", sad, and unhappy, they have got used to it and have accepted the lack of happiness as "a fact of life". When this has been going on for a long time, their low, unhappy vibration has become their point of attraction. And consequently they attract circumstances that are a vibrational match to their unhappy state of mind.

For that reason Abraham strongly advocates to get happy in any way you can. Do anything you can to get happy and find a reason to feel good. Do not allow unhappy thoughts to dominate your consciousness but make peace with where you are and start building your happiness from thoughts that feel good and give your individual attention to lovely things that you enjoy. You are the master of your thought sphere, so make sure that your thoughts match your dreams. It is so important to seek that good-feeling place because *"the disallowing of wellbeing creates illness"*. This means that if you allow yourself to accept an unhappy state of mind over a period of time, then you will create illness and unwanted circumstances. We can also put it like this: Every minute that you dwell on unhappy, sad and negative thoughts is a step towards something unwanted manifesting in your life. Consequently it is a good idea to learn to listen to your emotional guidance system and constantly try to become better at reaching out for happy thoughts and things to be pleased with.

What you get back from the universe is a vibrational match to what you have allowed to dominate your consciousness. The vibrational match to frustration and overwhelment could be headache, muscular pain and cramps, to anger and ill temper the vibrational match could be heart attack and to despair, fear and phobia it could be something serious like cancer. Serious illnesses are created when there is something in your life which really bothers you; it can be feelings of powerlessness, of not having control over your life, of being without influence, of being a victim etc.

But we were born with a "guidance system", a built-in compass, which gives us possibility for control, if only we would listen to it. So if we could learn to "read" our guidance system and be much more critical towards which unhappy thoughts and circumstances we accept, then we didn't have to create unwanted things in our lives.

It also means that it is highly recommendable to be critical about what you "feed" your vibration with. What you see, watch, observe, hear, read and let yourself be entertained by will all be included in your own vibration for a while. So when you watch a violent movie, listen to an irritating political debate, hear sad news etc, well, then you activate the corresponding vibration in your own vibration for a while, and that will affect your point of attraction. So a good idea would be to be careful about including too low vibrations in your own vibration. If you feel discomfort by what you are watching, well, then the emotional guidance system has passed judgment and it would be a good idea to change channels. If, on the other hand, you are watching a funny movie or a program that makes you rock with laughter, well, then you can go on, because the heightened vibration cannot attract other than pleasure, happiness and health.

Unfortunately there is a tendency to pay a lot of attention to things we don't like or get irritated with. But it is possible to move away from that habit simply by getting better at listening to what the emotional guidance system says. It would simply be desirable for us to get much better at reading our emotional guidance system, and we can get better at it when we actively decide that it is important to us how we feel. It would be a good idea to get much more "particular" about how we are feeling and only to accept feeling happy and content all of the time.

Of course, thinking happy thoughts is easier said than done, because even if we know that it is a good idea to choose a thought and thus a feeling that feels better than i.e. frustration, anger or powerlessness, then we may not always be able to find it and activate it in our vibration. But what one can try is to move up the emotional scale. If, for instance, you are depressed or in despair, it would feel better to be angry. It is possible to move upwards from mourning, fear, depression, despair, powerlessness, via uncertainty, blame, unworthiness, guilt, shame, via jealousy, hatred, fury, revenge, upset, worry, doubt, disappointment, frustration, irritation, pessimism to boredom, indifference, hopefulness, optimism, faith, expectation, and all the way up to satisfaction, enthusiasm, eagerness, passion, freedom, contentment, happiness, success and empowerment. The key to moving up the emotional scale is that you always try to reach out for a thought and an emotion that feels better than the one you had. And a little bit better is better than nothing, because from a better thought and feeling you can reach out for an even better thought and feeling and in that way you can move up the emotional scale.

For many people the easiest and quickest way to move up the emotional scale is to listen to music. Pick a piece of music that you really like, something that makes you jump around the room in a happy dance or float off into space in blissful reverie. It will lift you up the emotional scale very quickly. Also watching a funny movie or an entertaining program can lift you up, as can reading P.G. Wodehouse or Bill Bryson. Meditation is another way to move up, especially when you centre your thoughts on something empowering or simply dwell in the memory of the happiest moments of your life. Exercise is almost always helpful; it may be just a brisk walk in nature or a run around the block. The point is to make an active effort to move up the emotional scale and never accept being down without doing something active to get up again.

The aim of moving up the emotional scale is to reach a point where you are always content and happy about life. When you feel happy, content and in harmony, then you will attract everything that is a vibrational match to happiness, and that is health, wellbeing, abundance, success and everything you want. And the better it gets, the better it gets. Because the more happiness, contentment and joy you feel, the more happiness, contentment and joy will you attract.

Deactivation of Unwanted Thoughts

When your emotional guidance system has passed judgment and told you that this is a thought that gives bad feelings, well, then the question is: How to get rid of unwanted thoughts? Let us say that a thought about a cancerous growth is milling around in your head and even thought the emotional guidance system has told you to press delete, you cannot find the delete button. Your first reaction is probably to shout "no" and "go away" to the thought. But in an attraction based universe, it is not enough to shout "no", because the thought is still there, even though you are shouting "no" to it. Even though you shout "no" and "go away" to the thought, it is still the predominant thought in your consciousness, and consequently it is your point of attraction. If I tell you not to think about a pink elephant, then the first thing you do is to conjure up the image of a pink elephant in your mind. So "not" and "no" is not enough.

The only thing you can do to deactivate a certain thought is to activate another thought. So, if you don't want to think about a pink elephant, then you can activate another thought, i.e. you can think about a blue crocodile instead. The activation of the thought of the blue crocodile can deactivate the thought of the pink elephant. You can only get rid of an unwanted thought by activating a substitution thought in your consciousness.

This means that every time the thought of the cancerous growth or some other disease comes creeping in on you, you then must activate another and better thought in your consciousness. You must replace the thought of illness with a thought that can attract health and happiness. For instance, in your mind's eye, you can conjure up this image: you see yourself full of vigor and bubbling with health swinging in the lianas like Tarzan, then you jump into the river where you swim a few kilometers in a fast and powerful crawl and finally you end up in the arms of Jane and enjoy yourself with her in your leafy abode. It is highly likely that the latter string of thoughts will make you feel good, and consequently your inner guidance system has said OK to the thoughts. You can always replace a thought about illness with a thought about health, you can always replace a thought about failure with a thought about success and you can always replace a thought about fear with a thought about hope.

Or put in another way: You can only delete a particular thought from the hard disk by replacing the file with another file. An actual delete function does not exist.

You are the ruler of your thoughts, they don't rule over you. The first step in the direction of achieving a better mix of thoughts is the realization that you call the shots. Your thoughts don't. You decide what to think. This realization is both liberating and empowering.

But compulsory thoughts can be hard to get rid of, and again it is through practice that you become a master. For every inappropriate thought you have, you should establish a substitution thought. If you have established a substitution thought to the thought of cancer (for instance by thinking about the happiest moment in your life) and you have been successful in activating this wonderful moment a number of times, when the thought of cancer came sneaking up, well then it is as if the cancer thought gradually gets tired of the game and finally stops turning up all together. Establishing and activating substitution thoughts is actually an effective way of getting rid of unwanted thoughts. When you visualize a pleasant and empowering thought every time the compulsory thought pops up, thus pushing the undesired thought away, then it is my experience that the compulsory thought will subside in just a few days. And as always: the more you practice the better you get at controlling your thoughts.

If you cannot get away from the thought about your house being burgled, well, then again it is a good idea to establish an alternative thought. Instead of seeing burglars on their way into your villa, you can visualize 100 fat, little angels, who on their small wings fly around the house in order to look after it. Or you can visualize a whole legion of Roman soldiers keeping watch in front of the house, making sure that no burglar gets near it. If you cannot stop worrying about your children, it is a good idea to visualize them healthy, happy, competent, smart, clever, successful etc.

Never, never, never dwell on thoughts that make you feel antipathy or discomfort. Quickly deactivate any unpleasant thought and replace it with a pleasant one. In that way you have made yourself an "attractor" or magnet of good occurrences, events and people.

Attraction Catalysts

The more joy, passion and enthusiasm we apply to our thoughts, the stronger our point of attraction is. We can put it like this: our enthusiastic display of emotions in connection with a thought object will make the object materialize in our life quickly.

In Abraham's words: *"The thoughts that you think without bringing forth the feeling of strong emotion are not of great magnetic power. In other words, while every thought that you think has creative potential or magnetic attraction potential, the thoughts that are thought in combination with the feeling of strong emotion are the most powerful".* (The Law of Attraction, page 40).

Our enthusiasm simply feeds the thought with so much energy that it will attract the object faster than if the enthusiasm was lacking. So if we want to attract a certain thing or event quickly, then it is recommendable that we start by feeling happy about the impending manifestation of the object. We should anticipate our happiness about possessing what we want. It also helps raising your arms, jumping around in triumph and performing a happy, little dance. The more passion, the stronger the attraction.

But in the same way as passionate enthusiasm works as a catalyst for the realization of your wishes, also passionate rejection, hatred, fear or despair work as catalysts. In a universe where attraction is the fundamental principle, you will attract everything that you have strong feelings about. Both passionate happiness and passionate rejection feed extra energy into your thoughts, and the extra energy makes sure that the object will manifest quickly in your life.

So what you fear with passionate rejection, be it assault, theft, rape, accidents or illness, you will attract quickly in the same way as you will attract what you passionately want quickly. Attraction is attraction and the law of attraction cannot distinguish between wanted and unwanted objects. We simply attract what we focus on. It is not the job of the law to "clean up" our attraction, it is our own job. The law works as it always does: all the time and without exception.

Examples of Inappropriate Attraction

One of the best examples in recent times of inappropriate attraction is probably the case of an unfortunate watchmaker in Copenhagen, whose small shop had been assaulted seven times within a short span of time. Nobody could explain why this precise watchmaker should be so unfortunate, but it is the law of attraction that is at work. The watchmaker had been worried about his shop and had begun fearing that it would be burgled. With thoughts of fear and worry you attract what you worry about. Every day the watchmaker worried about burglary and visualized vividly how burglars and attackers broke into his shop to steal his vintage watches. By thinking this thought repeatedly, he attracted the burglary. This is neither mystery nor mumbo jumbo, but it is quite simply a natural law that now decrees that the shop must be burgled. The burglary has been attracted, indeed "ordered", by the owner of the shop through his focusing on burglary.

After the first burglary the owner gets upset and he now focuses with passionate anger and rejection on the burglary. And when you focus on something with passion, you attract it even faster and with more power. With his passionate rejection of the idea of burglary, the watchmaker attracts even more burglary. In that way he starts an evil cycle. The more burglaries, the more passionate rejection. But a passionate rejection of burglary is still a focused thought and consequently an attractor of burglary. You don't deactivate a thought about burglary by shouting "NO" at it. So the burglaries continue until the day when the watchmaker has had enough and therefore buys a gun for what he thinks is his own protection. Now he is standing there is his shop foaming with anger with his gun, "ready" to receive the attackers. In this way he has attracted them with even more power and look: they come to burgle the shop, he shoots and the case has an unfortunate ending for him: he is accused of assault and illegal possession of arms.

The watchmaker has activated the law of attraction in the most effective way, i.e. by thinking and consequently attracting in a focused and passionate way. It is no chance that he is burgled and attacked all those times, it is just the law of attraction in action. But the poor man didn't know that and consequently he unknowingly created undesired and fatal circumstances for himself.

In order to have avoided the attacks the watchmaker should have thought safety. He should, for instance, have visualized his shop surrounded by a tall security fence, a tall wall of concrete, 100 police officers, 50 German shepherds, 70 guardian angels, a thick barrier of bricks, a barricade of pallets and boxes – no matter what, as long as it was something that could deactivate the thought of the attacks.

The more passionately you think about something, the stronger you attract it. Passionate wishes "fired up" by expectation, happiness, and joy will be attracted much faster than tame, lazy wishes. In the same way thoughts "fired up" by a passionate rejection or fear will be attracted fast. It means that if you are passionately afraid of contracting a certain illness, say breast cancer, and you allow your thoughts to revolve around this with great frequency and passion and shout "no" to the thought loud and clear, well then you are well on the road to being given the diagnosis of breast cancer. What you focus on with passion you attract quickly. But fortunately you can stop the attraction of breast cancer by focusing on total health and by eliminating every thought about illness from your thought sphere.

As mentioned, we are quite often not aware of which form of attraction we emit. For instance, it is not unusual to see that women, who for years have been living with violent men, in spite of the bad experiences, still link up with another violent man as soon as they have got rid of the first one. It has often been a source of wonder why these women could not learn from their experience and avoid entering into relationships where there would just be "more of the same". But this is due to the fact that they have not changed their attraction, and that mainly means their thought pattern, before they entered into a new relationship. They are quite simply so used to being repressed, subjugated and violated, and their self esteem is so low, that they no longer believe that they can find a loving husband. They have unknowingly set their vibration so low that we are talking about inappropriate attraction. They have long ago stopped listening to their inner guidance system, which would have told them that they were off course, if they only had paid attention. But they are deaf to their guidance system and their point of attraction is now so low and full of acceptance of being a victim that they soon attract another violent partner. Only by changing the way they think about themselves and the way they visualize relationships, can they change their point of attraction. It quite simply takes a strong "remodeling of the thought sphere" to change their attraction. And this remodeling can best be brought about if they decide that it is important for them how they feel, and that they are happy and content.

Your Life is Your Own Responsibility

It should have become clear from the above that whatever we have in our lives is our own responsibility. Through our choice of thoughts we have attracted everything that we have in our lives. It is no good blaming others if our lives are not the way we want. Nobody but we are responsible for our lives.

However, nor should we blame ourselves, if we are not content with what we have manifested. Or put in another way: Your life is your own responsibility, but it is not your fault. If you have attracted unwanted circumstances, illnesses or calamities in your life, you most certainly did not do this on purpose. You probably did it because you did not know any better. You were ignorant about the workings of the law of attraction, so you dwelt on the undesired "by default" and attracted things and happenings that were not to your liking. We can say that ignorance about the workings of the law of attraction is responsible for the unwanted things.

But when you become aware of the importance of the law of attraction and the way it works, then you must take full responsibility for your life and do what you can to attract the wanted. Then there is no excuse, and you have the best possible instrument that will help you choose what is best for you: your emotional guidance system. And remember: there is no failure, only feedback. Learn from your experiences and never beat yourself up. Make peace with where you are, accept yourself and decide to move forward. Decide that from now you are going to create deliberately.

Examples of Appropriate Attraction

There are innumerable examples that the law of attraction works. A few will be mentioned here. Many of the examples are from my own life, as they are the ones I have the easiest access to.

We had a patient who needed an implant put in by the surgeon we use. The appointment had been made, but then the surgeon called our clinic in order to change the time. But our patient didn't have a telephone and he only had an incomplete address. There was no way that we could contact him. But we didn't think that we could let him drive the 100 km. to the surgeon in vain, so now what to do? My husband and I looked at each other and said: we need help from the powers above. The following Saturday morning we had a sudden impulse to go to Almuñecar. We went down to the market and just outside the entrance we bumped into our patient. *"Oh, how fortunate, we have an important message for you"*. The patient then explained that suddenly, as he was building a brick wall (he is a brick layer) he had an impulse to go to Almuñecar, something he normally never did on a Saturday. Anyway, we met and the problem was solved. I can only ascribe this solution to the law of attraction which effected that we both acted on a sudden impulse so that we could meet.

One of our friends was a member of a well-known Danish rock band in the 70s. He had noticed something that he found strange. When in certain periods all the members of the band were busy with other things and could find no time to perform, then there were no calls from organizers and no engagements. But then, when again they had time to play and started thinking that now they would like to have some engagements, then the phones started ringing and the bookings were pouring in. None of the members of the band could understand how this happened, but it was the law of attraction in action. You manifest what you think about.

One of our acquaintances had done me a favor, and I had decided that I would give him three bottles of red wine in return. But now a few weeks had passed, and I still hadn't got around to buying the bottles, so I started having a bad conscience. On Sunday night I thought that I would get it done on Monday. When I came to work on Monday morning there was a package with three bottles of red wine waiting for me, nicely wrapped with colored ribbons. The only thing I needed to do was to replace the card from the sender with one of my own. It seemed to me as if I had had a very competent sub manager who had carried out my order, because it had been carried out to the letter. Abraham says that we can view the law of attraction as a willing employee, who carries out all our orders.

One day I was sitting at my desk in our summer house writing. Our drive was completely overgrown and several times we had been saying that we needed to do something to get rid of all the grass and weeds. But that was as far as we had got. While I'm sitting there the man, who usually cuts our lawn, suddenly appears. He comes in and says: *"Did you not want your drive attended to?"* *"Yes, but I haven't told anybody, so how do you know?"* *"Well, I think I heard somewhere"*. Hum, I thought – this works as by telepathy. The fact is we had our drive cleared without having to do other than wish it was done.

Mike Dooley, author and lecturer, tells a funny story about how he, before he became an author, dreamt about traveling. He had received a post card from Hong Kong, showing a fantastic view of the South Chinese Sea. Mike pinned the post card on the wall and thought that this was the exact view he would like to see and experience. Some months passed and Mike had a new job which involved a certain amount of traveling. On one of his trips he was one day standing by the window in a Hong Kong hotel and to his great surprise he realized that it was exactly the view that was on his post card, that he was now looking at. Not a view that resembled the one on the post card, but exactly the same. It was at that precise moment that Mike decided to write books on the law of attraction.

My husband and I had been talking about getting two new television sets, because the old ones needed replacing and we had been saying that we would like to have two new flat screens. We had been discussing this while traveling, and the idea was to look at new television screens when we got home. The day after we got home somebody rang the door and outside there was a delivery man with two flat packages for us. We had no idea what it was, nor who had sent them, so we were very surprised when the packages turned out to contain two brand new Philips flat screens. The sender turned out to be our bank and the present was some sort of bonus.

Then there is the story about the entrepreneur who had pinned a photo of his dream house on his notice board. Every day he looked at the photo and wanted to live in just that house. Now things happened in his life which meant that he had to move around a lot, so he packed his things into boxes, including the notice board with the photo of the dream house. Five years passed and the entrepreneur had been quite successful, so now he had bought a big house, which he had renovated. The house was ready to move into and when he unpacks his things after five years and sees the photo of his dream house, he realizes in all its amazing glory that the house which he has bought, renovated and now is living in, is the house on the photo. Not a house like it, but exactly the same house. He had bought his dream house without knowing it. The law of attraction had seen to it that he had been attracted to the house the wanted the most. (9)

On the day of Christmas Eve 2007 we were sitting with two of our children at the breakfast table in the summer house discussing geography. We agreed that we had some kind of duty to know the geography of the world. In order to test our knowledge we set ourselves the task to list the countries of Africa and the states of the USA. It went quite well, but we couldn't remember them all. Now, obviously, the need arose to look them up in an atlas or encyclopedia, but in the summerhouse we did not have a geographical work of reference. This is too bad, we agreed. Ten (!) minutes passed, and then the book we wanted came walking right into our living room. Our eldest daughter came with our Christmas presents, took one quick look at what we were doing and pulled a book titled "Geographica" out of her bag. The book had world maps and all the information we needed. It was a belated birthday present for me.

I'll end this chapter with another fantastic example from my own life. I had decided to subscribe to a certain "news letter" via the Internet. I had to type in name, address etc., and then I would get a number code back from the firm, which I was to use when I wanted to log on. Now, I always use the same code for everything. Let us say that it is: 4467. But I hadn't informed the organization in question about my code, because they hadn't asked me for one. Consequently I was so taken aback that I nearly fell off the chair, when the following code a few seconds later appeared on my screen: 44675. I had received my usual code, but because they operated with 5 digits, I had a 5 in the end. I actually have no words to express how overwhelmed, surprised, taken aback and grateful I was that it was at all possible that I could get my own code back without having informed it. I can only ascribe the "mystery" to the law of attraction.

The examples mentioned here suggest that there might be a "mechanism" in the Universe that makes our wishes come true. Can it really be so? Wouldn't it be fantastic if it were so?

This is what we'll explore in the next chapter.

6. Wishes and Longings

Our wishes are also thoughts and now the question presents itself: Will our wishes come true? Is there any point at all in wishing anything? Probably many people think that it doesn't matter what they wish for, because it is never going to come true anyway. But that is not so! Our universe has been construed so that our wishes <u>must</u> come true. It is simply a natural law, because everything in the universe goes in circles. And because wishes and longings are energies that we send out into the universe, these energies will, sooner or later, return to us, their point of departure. It is this interesting aspect that we shall look upon in this chapter.

The Compass of Life

As we are eternal beings on a fascinating journey through time and space and through spiritual spheres beyond time and space, it is obvious that there has to be a compass that can determine the course for this long, long journey. We can put it like this: the goal of the journey has been determined by the board of directors above, or by the Source or Godhead, if you like. The goal of the journey is to become an all-loving being that lives in peace and harmony with others. In well-known words the goal is to become "man in the image and likeness of God". A human being in the likeness of God is a being that radiates universal love to all other beings, be they plants, animals or humans. Such a being cannot hate, judge or kill and s/he lives to serve others and is altruistic in everything that s/he thinks or does.

It is the goal for all us travelers to become such an all-loving being. So the goal of our journey has been decided for us. We cannot escape this goal or choose another one. But it is our own choice how we reach the goal. We can say that it is up to us to decide which route to take to the goal. We have free will to decide for ourselves which way to go. It is obvious that this journey takes many, many incarnations, indeed the physical part of the journey begins in the mineral kingdom in order then to move through the plant- and animal kingdoms and into the human kingdom. Martinus points out that most earthlings of today are unfinished human beings with varying degrees of animal (egoistic) mentality left. But the animal mentality is being cleansed and eradicated for each incarnation that we live and in tune with our experience of life and our sufferings. Martinus says that the physical world is a work-shop where the real, altruistic human being is under creation. We can also say that we are works of art under construction.

Martinus also points out that not everybody has reached the same level of development in the process of becoming real human beings. We are quite simply standing on different steps of the ladder towards perfection. We aren't finished yet, but we're not all equally unfinished. It is clear that those who can no longer hate, slander, boast, wound and kill are more "finished" than those who can still find it in their hearts to do those things. It is clear that a human being, who has no scruples in killing another human being to get an advantage, stands below a peace loving being, who couldn't dream of hurting or killing. But Martinus also underlines that everybody will reach this grand goal. There is nobody who will not, sooner or later, become man in the image and likeness of God. The goal is clear and we cannot avoid getting there. It is only a question of which route we take and then, of course, of when we get there. In about 3000 years enough of us will have reached the point where we are real human beings, free from all egoistic tendencies, and then a realm of peace will arise on Earth, says Martinus. In such a world kingdom of peace all poverty, inequality, war, murder, intolerance and egoism will have been eradicated and we will all live in harmony and happiness.

The great goal of our life's journey has already been determined, but which route should we take, then? Should we take the hazardous route over the Timmelsjoch pass or the easier one over the Brenner Pass to get from Munich to Rome? Should we take the sandy route through the Sahara or sail up the Nile to get to Luxor? Should we fly or drive to Paris? That is completely up to us. And to advise us in these choices we have a built-in compass, which tells us what to choose: our emotional guidance system and our wishes and desires.

Our wishes are the offspring of the primordial desire. Martinus defines the primordial desire as the inherent desire for life that all living beings have. The primordial desire is the driving force that drives us forward, and we can say that our individual wishes and desires are the details that each and every one of us dresses the primordial desire in. This detailing has its root in the principle of hunger and satiation.

Hunger and Satiation

Hunger and satiation is a principle which we all know in connection with our food. When we are hungry, we have a desire to eat, and when we are full, then the desire has been satiated. We can satiate our desire for food by eating fish and chips every day, but after some time we will have reached a point where we cannot stand the sight of more fish and chips. Then our desire shifts towards some other kind of food. The principle of hunger and satiation dictates that what we have eaten a large amount of times will eventually make us so satiated that we cannot stand the sight of it anymore, and a new hunger towards a new type of food arises.

But this principle is absolutely fundamental and reaches far beyond the area of food. It is at the root of our basic driving force and desire for experience of life. When we have experienced a specific situation a certain amount of times, we become satiated with this situation and a hunger for a new situation with a new type of experience arises. We quite simply long for a contrasting experience to the situations that we have experienced "ad nauseam" and this "mechanism" is driven by the principle of hunger and satiation. Martinus expresses it like this:

"The Principle of Hunger and Satiation"

"The driving forces behind all experience of life are desire, wishes and longings. Without desires the form of life which characterizes Mankind today would never have arisen and likewise there would be no future for Mankind if their consciousness wasn't filled with wishes and longings. That every normal, natural wish will come true, is not what human beings believe, because they don't know the laws of life and don't know that <u>every wish sets a cycle in motion, which has its beginning in a longing for something and does not stop until this longing has been satisfied.</u> They do, however, know this from their relationship to food; they get hungry for food and this desire is satiated by them getting something to eat... However, hunger and satiation is not something that relates solely to the physical food. All types of desire, wishes and longings are in principle exactly the same. Just as the hunger for food cannot stop until it is somehow satisfied, this is also valid for all the other types of desire, longings and wishes within our consciousness". (Martinus: "Longing", Kosmos 2, 2003, my underlining added.)

It is quite a revelation that Martinus offers here, because he says that all our wishes will come true. When it is like that, it is because everything in the universe moves in cycles, and the cycle of a desire can only be completed when the desire has been fulfilled or come true.

"The Cycle of Wishes

Many people would protest against such a thought with the motivation that they have many wishes and desires that have never come true. They are disappointed and may even feel let down by life, because now they have grown old without their wishes having come true. The fact that people can grow old without their longings and wishes having come true, apparently does not fit well with the idea that all wishes and longings must come true. <u>But it is only apparently so. It is because people still only see their life in a small, local</u>

perspective, that starts at conception and birth and ends at death. They think that their life is like a straight line with a beginning and an ending. But this "straight line " is, like all other straight lines, only an illusion. The straight line does not really exist. Any line is an expression of force or energy and all energy in the universe goes in cycles." (Ibid).

What Martinus says here is that a wish or a longing is an energy that we send out into the universe and this energy must, like everything else, describe a cycle as no movement in the universe can go in a straight line.

Because the longing has been sent out it must necessarily, as defined by a natural law, describe a cyclic movement and this cycle can only stop when it has completed its obligatory circular course. And when the energy returns to its point of departure, the longing will be neutralized. And this neutralizing can only take place when the longing is fulfilled. This fulfillment is a prerequisite for the completion of the cycle. And this completion takes place in exactly the same way as when our physical hunger can only be satisfied when we get something to eat. The completion can only take place by the fulfillment of the wish. For that reason it has nothing to do with luck or fortunate circumstances that our wishes come true. It is a natural law that they **must** come true.

When many people don't experience that their wishes come true, there can be various reasons for this. Martinus points out that the fulfillment of the wish can take place in a future incarnation, so that the wish will come true in one's next life or maybe in a life that is further ahead. One thing is for sure: the wish will come true, because the cycle must be completed. It is law.

We should also have a quick look at the following interesting passage from the above quotation:

"Without desires the form of life which characterizes Mankind today would never have arisen and likewise there would be no future for Mankind, if their consciousness wasn't filled with wishes and longings."

Here Martinus draws our attention to a very fundamental aspect of our wishes and longings, viz. that it is the desires of Man that shape the future, just as it is the desires of past generations that have shaped the times that we are now living in. It is the past generations' desires about an improved way of life that we are now enjoying, because without a desire about improvements in one's life they cannot come about. The thought always comes before the physical manifestation.

The thought and the consequential mental picture of a chair always comes before the physical chair, the thought about a vehicle that can drive on its own, without a horse, comes before the invention of the physical car, the thought of being able to fly in the air like the bird comes before the physical airplane etc. All the manmade things that we see in our world have been a thought before they became physical manifestations. All of it, no exceptions. This again means that the whole of our civilization is manifested thoughts; it is the wishes and desires of past generations that have come true. We shall look deeper into this interesting aspect in the second part of the book.

So, Martinus says that it is a natural law that our wishes shall come true. It is our "I", the core of our perception of having a "self", which, like a magician, juggles with the energies.

"As mentioned earlier in "Livets Bog" all matter can be traced back to the six major basic energies of instinct, gravity, feeling, intelligence, intuition and memory. These fundamental basic energies exist as sources of power for the "I" that exists in every living being. These energies are so closely related to the "I" that it only has to wish, and the energies will immediately be put into motion, indeed, even the smallest, most microscopic desire will make these energies enter into different combinations. As I have mentioned before, the "I" sits on "the divine throne" completely raised above all energies. These lie like obedient, serving forces below it, meant to be used whenever it fits into the being of the "I". (Martinus: Livets Bog II, paragraph 326).

Our "I" is the sovereign ruler in our spiritual body and hence also in our physical body, and as soon as the "I" has expressed even the smallest desire, energies are put in motion in order to fulfill the expressed desire. The energies lie like serving forces below the "I" and it means, as already mentioned, that every wish moves towards its fulfillment. This happens because, as soon as the wish has been expressed, energies have been put in motion that forward the fulfillment of the wish. And the more we focus on our wish, the more power it gets, and the more passionate power we give it, the sooner it will happen. *"Your wish is my command"*, as the genie in Aladdin's lamp says, is much more than fantasy. Getting what we want is not an expression of naïve wishful thinking, but is conditioned by the law of movement (everything moves in cycles) and the law of attraction. It is on the basis of these principles that our universe has been organized.

To Focus on the Fulfillment of the Wish

Abraham totally agrees that all our wishes will come true, because it is determined by the law of attraction that everything that we attract with our thoughts and wishes will manifest. *"What you think, feel and focus on and what manifests is always a match. Every time. No exception."*

But Abraham has an important addition to make on the subject of making one's wishes come true. When you want to have your wish fulfilled, it is a prerequisite that you are in energetic alignment with the fulfillment of the wish. What does that mean? It means that your own vibration must be on wavelength with the fulfillment or realization of the wish. It again means that you should not obstruct the fulfillment of your wishes by not believing that they will ever come true or by focusing on the lack of materialization of the fulfillment of the wish, or by being full of fear that your wishes won't come true. Your focusing on lack, fear and disappointment will prevent the fulfillment of your wishes, because the energy of lack, fear and disappointment is not a vibrational match to the fulfillment of the wishes. Let us look at an example:

You want to find a perfect boyfriend, this really good looking stud that you have always been dreaming about. When you close your eyes, you can see him clearly in your mind. But as you are looking at him in all his glory, doubt comes creeping and you think: I'm not good enough for him, he is way too attractive for me, he would probably rather be with my beautiful cousin, I'll never get married, and my teeth are too big and by legs are too short etc., etc. With these thoughts, which vibrationally are not in alignment with the fulfillment of the wish, you effectively close off the possibility of your wish coming true. Negativity, fear and worry are not a vibrational match or on vibrational wavelength with the fulfillment of the wish, so thoughts of doubt and worry will prevent you from getting what you want.

What you have to do to let the fulfillment in, is to think positively of it and be happy about it. Instead of focusing on the wish not having come true yet, you have to think fulfillment, abundance and the actual coming true of the wish. In the example from above you should already feel the joy of walking up the aisle to marry your dream guy.

The best way to bring your thoughts in vibrational alignment with the fulfillment of the wish is to see it in your mind's eye as already fulfilled. By doing so and by already feeling pleased that your wish has come true, you have brought yourself in vibrational alignment with the fulfillment. When you believe that the wish will come true and are already taking pleasure in it, then the law of attraction will see to it that the energy can flow freely into your aura and it will not be obstructed. You yourself can really contribute to the fulfillment of your wishes by letting your heart flow over with joy and gratitude for the fulfillment, indeed it helps if you dance around in happiness, stretch your arms in the air and shout "yes!" and "hurrah!". Then the energy can flow freely and it will not meet any type of obstruction.

If, on the other hand, you focus on the lack of the fulfillment of the wish, you have blocked the possibility of its coming true. You have, because your focusing on the lack is not in vibrational alignment with the fulfillment of the wish. It means that when the cycle of the wish is complete and it is "sitting right outside your front door" it cannot come in because the wavelength of your aura is too "foreign" to the wavelength of the wish. You see, the law of attraction and repulsion dictates that dissimilar wavelengths repel each other, so unless you have brought your thoughts on wavelength with the fulfillment of the wish, you cannot let it in. The fulfillment of the wish is then "parked" right outside your front door until you have brought your vibration on wavelength with the fulfillment of the wish. You must find the key to letting in the fulfillment of your dream by letting your thoughts sore to the height they had when you dreamt your dream.

Abraham says that there is an endless amount of wishes that are thus waiting "in vibrational escrow" right outside your front door, waiting for you to let them in vibrationally. "Close the gap", say Abraham, and with this they mean that you must work constantly at reducing the vibrational dissimilarity between your own vibration and the vibration of your wishes. As soon as you have "closed the gap", the realization of the wishes can flow to you freely, and the best way to "close the gap" is to be full of positive expectation and happiness.

There are innumerable examples of people who wish very strongly for something, but cannot make the wishes come true because they focus on the lack, on the absence of the fulfillment.

Innumerable couples who want to conceive a child cannot make the desired pregnancy a reality no matter how much they try. And when they don't succeed it is, in many cases, because they focus on the lack of the pregnancy. They focus on sperm count and temperature curves, on fertility tests and dates of ovulation, and all this makes them centre their thoughts on the lack of the wanted conception. And when they focus on the lack, they cannot let the fulfillment in energetically. It cannot be done, because their wavelength of lack does not harmonize with the fulfillment of the wish – the two energies are too dissimilar and repulsion takes place. It is then often the case that as soon as they adopt a child and hold this child in their arms, then they no longer focus on the absence of a child (as there now *is* a child) and thus they bring their energy on wavelength with their wish for a child. And then the miracle happens: they conceive a child.

If you are looking for a boyfriend you may have experienced periods of drought: not a boyfriend in sight. When you then finally (by focusing positively on his presence in your life) find the desired boyfriend, you suddenly run into a shoal of boyfriends: they call you, you get e-mails, you are invited out and are suddenly the centre of attention from several potential boyfriends. Why? Because you have closed the gab, and are now on vibrational alignment with the fulfillment of your wish.

You cannot manifest anything by focusing on its vibrational opposite. Only by focusing on the fulfillment of the wish and already feeling happy that it is on its way, can you let the fulfillment of your wishes in. This has nothing to do with chance and nothing to do with luck or fortune. It is law. It is the strongest natural law of the universe that dictates that only energies that are on wavelength can attract each other. And if you focus on lack, it is as impossible to attract the fulfillment of your wish as it is impossible for you to receive a radio station on 108,4 FM if you tune your radio receiver to 99,8 FM. It cannot be done. It is contrary to a natural law.

Gratitude

What can you do, if you are uncertain if you are a good "magnet" for the fulfillment of your wishes?

One thing is certain: you don't get anywhere near the fulfillment of your wishes if you are angry, bitter and dissatisfied with life. Anger and bitterness attract energies on the same wavelength and consequently you attract more anger and bitterness. Some people feel unjustly treated by life and see themselves as martyrs, as scapegoats for the unkind whims of fate and as totally innocent victims of a giant cosmic plot to annoy them. *"It is not my fault, it is all the others who are out to get me"*, they say and they lift their fist to heaven in a threatening gesture and damn the universe and everything in it.

Let it be said right away: that attitude does not lead anywhere desirable; it only leads to more martyrdom, pessimism and depression. That attitude just attracts more energies on the same wavelength and thus you will have started a spiral of misery, unhappiness and "poor me". The spiral can only be broken by a change of thoughts through which you change your vibration and consequently your attraction.

A really good place to start is to begin focusing on things or circumstances to be grateful about. Thoughts of gratitude immediately change your vibration and thus your attraction in a very decisive way. Thoughts of gratitude make you attract much better energies than thoughts of pessimism, depression and dissatisfaction. Practicing thoughts of gratitude is a very good place to start, if you think that things don't go your way. If you look around, you will always be able to find things to be grateful about. They can be simple things such as having a good bed to sleep in, having water that pours out of the tap, having food to satiate your hunger, having clothes to wear, being able to turn the heat up and down, being able to be entertained by magazines, books, radio, television, movies, and theatre, having a good friend, having sunshine, watching an apple tree in bloom, smelling a rose, seeing the green grass etc.

Once you have found one thing to be grateful for, you can find even more, and when you consciously look for things to be grateful for, you activate more positive vibrations, which attract positive occurrences, which again attract even more positive vibrations and occurrences. And with your accumulation of thoughts of gratitude you can start an avalanche of "good vibes", positive things happening and a good "feed back" from your surroundings. In that way you will have brought your vibration on a good wavelength, where you can start attracting the things and circumstances you want.

Once you have lifted your vibration from martyrdom to gratitude, it will be easier for you to lift it even higher to satisfaction, optimism, eagerness, passion, happiness, joy, freedom, love and enthusiasm. And when you reach enthusiasm, then you are completely on wavelength with the fulfillment of your wishes. When you already feel the joy of the fulfillment of the wishes, well, then you have opened the front door wide and the fulfillment of your wishes can flow freely to you. Then there is no energetic discrepancy between the wish and its fulfillment, and the moment you change the wavelength of your radiation from martyrdom and "it's everybody else's fault", you will very soon see the results in your life. You will then be met by energies that match your own, and life will begin to smile at you. And the better it is, the better it gets, because "joy de vivre" attracts more circumstances to feel happy about. You can simply start a spiral of happiness that can only lead upwards towards more gratitude, happiness and satisfaction with life.

The Journey from Birmingham to London

Abraham illustrates the process for the realization of one's wishes in the following way: We can imagine that we have a deep wish to get a job in the Foreign Office. In our thoughts we maintain a mental picture of ourselves working at a specific post in the Foreign Office. We can compare our present position (no job in the Foreign Office) and our goal (a job in the Foreign Office) with a journey from Birmingham to London.

As we all know there are many ways to get from Birmingham to London. You can fly, go by train, go by bus, go by car, motorcycle, moped, bicycle and you can even walk. It doesn't matter which of the above mentioned means of transportation you choose, because as long as you stick to the decision that London is your goal, well, then you will eventually arrive in London. It is only a question of how long it takes.

But if, when you are passing Oxford, it suddenly occurs to you that you would like to go to the Cotswolds, well, then London is no longer your goal, and consequently you have "cancelled" the realization of your project. It can then be so that you hang around in the Cotswolds for an amount of time, until you remember that, oh, it was London that was your goal. When again you focus on getting to London, then you will eventually get there.

The same principle applies to the realization of our wishes. As long as we maintain a mental picture of the job in the Foreign Office, well, then it is as certain that we will get it, as it is that we will get to London if we set our compass for that city. But if, during the process, we decide to make do with a job in the municipal treasurer's department of Hawick and forget about the wish to work in the Foreign Office, then the wish cannot come true. We must, without hesitation, keep a firm mental picture of our goal and "keep the door open" for the realization of the goal by focusing on its fulfillment. In other words we should believe in it and rejoice that it is coming true. Joyful expectation together with constant focusing on the goal will always bring the desire result. The law of attraction sees to that.

It is valid for the coming true of any wish that activity on your part forwards the process. You can lie on the sofa and focus on the realization of your wishes, but they will come true faster, if your activities take you in the same direction. Just as diligence is the mother of luck, we can say that focused activity helps the realization of our wishes along. Or said in another way: the universe helps the person who helps himself. And it works like this because our own activity strengthens our focusing and thus we become stronger attractors. Focused activity could be anything that brings you closer to your goal: studying, searching the internet, sending out applications, sending out letters of introduction, distributing flyers etc. Anything that keeps you focused on your goal will forward the coming true of your wish.

However, you reach the goal of your wishes faster by thinking the right thoughts than by working harder. And when you have reached the point when you work out of joy, and consequently your work does not feel like work, but like a game that you would play anyway, then you have become a super attractor of everything you wish. Those who have become really successful through their own activities are those who were having fun at the same time.

Choice of Thoughts

You quite simply change your reality through your choice of thoughts. The world is as you think it. There may be an outer world that behaves in a certain way, but it is your own choice of thoughts around what happens that is of importance to you. Every event can be interpreted in various ways, and it is up to you to choose how to interpret what happens and what importance you want it to have for you. Nobody but you can make this choice. Nobody but you can see the world through your eyes.

And when you know that what you focus on becomes your reality because focused thoughts invariably will be manifested, well then you are well on your way to discovering your own incredible power over your life. That power is your birth right, but perhaps you gave that power up somewhere along the way from either ignorance or disbelief in it. Or maybe you just prefer to not think about yourself as so enormously powerful. The enormous power may scare you and you may not want to own so much power, but whether you want to or not −

you still own it. And one thing is certain: owning that amount of power deprives you of the right to blame others for the way your life enfolds. There is only you to think your thoughts and only you to do the attracting in your life. No one else can attract in your energy field. Only you.

Mental Woundology

It is not unusual to hear people say that they cannot achieve anything in life because they, for instance, had an unhappy childhood. Because their father beat them or their mother was an alcoholic, or they were neglected or abused, well, then nothing can be done, because their lives have already been ruined. They choose to focus on the wounds of the past; indeed, they have with time become very masterful at cultivating their mental wounds and will, at any given opportunity, show them to the world and project their pain up on the wall. This projection of pain can easily become a pretext for doing nothing, a gigantic excuse not to get on with life. Indeed, it can come to the extreme that every day, when they wake up, they send a stream of thoughts down to the wounds of the past. When you send a stream of thoughts down to the past, you simultaneous send a stream of life force down to the same past. Because thoughts are life force. When you send your life force down to old wounds, well, then you have less life force left for today and the now. To hang on to old injuries is some of the most negative activity you can practice. It will ruin your present day life and your future. It will, because thinking of yourself as a martyr is the worst imaginable life strategy. Martinus says:

"[The depressed person] sees only hopelessness and more hopelessness. He finds everything insurmountable to the extent that it makes him feel an over-dimensioned pity or commiseration with himself. He feels a martyr. He feels a victim to the whims of nature, if it isn't other people he blames for his "martyrdom". It is obvious that this situation will lead to depression if it isn't stopped. But depression is again the beginning of insanity, which in the worst case can lead to suicide. A human being cannot get more abnormal than that". (Martinus: "Unnatural fatigue", chapter 2, booklet no. 16).

With thoughts of martyrdom you magnetize your blood negatively and such a negative magnetization will sooner or later lead to illness and depression.

"As all thoughts are radiated force, which not only radiates and is directed through the brain, but also radiates through the atomic- or micro structure in both the blood, the muscles and the nerves, it is of major importance which type of thoughts go through the micro life and organs of the organism: As happy thoughts constitute the normal life force in the animal organism, the life force is destroyed to the same extent as the human being is filled with thoughts of

anger, depression and martyrdom". (Martinus: "Unnatural Fatigue", chapter 9, booklet no. 16, my underlining added).

Happy thoughts constitute the normal life force for the human organic structure, and this is a very important point to underline. In order for the organism to function optimally, be healthy, well and functional, it takes happy thoughts. Any deviation from happy thoughts will sooner or later create illness. For that reason it is of major importance that we seek to abstain from focusing on old wounds, martyrdom and "poor me". We can abstain from this by choosing our thoughts differently. Every time thoughts of martyrdom come sneaking in, we can practice activating a different and more positive thought. It could for instance be a thought of what we in our wildest dreams would want to happen in our lives, it could be wishes about wealth, popularity, abundance and "joi de vivre". The more we focus on the wanted things, and the more we can do this with conviction, gratitude, happiness and belief that it will materialize, the faster they come.

Abraham insists again and again that we shouldn't make a big, hairy deal out of the wounds from the past. If we have a tendency to do this, we can choose to change focus and concentrate our thoughts on something better. To the past we can just say "so what". It doesn't matter where you were yesterday, or which thoughts you thought last week, because the most important thing is where you have your vibration right now, and how you are feeling right now. Your point of attraction is the now. The better you can make your vibration here and now, and the better you feel, the better circumstances will you attract into your life. And you can change your vibration and get on with your life by changing focus. You don't have to change anything in your external circumstances – by choosing better thoughts and happier feelings, the outer circumstances will follow suit. And the better it gets, the better it gets. Better thoughts attract even better thoughts, better thoughts attract better circumstances – it all just gets better and better.

Make peace with your past and with yourself. Never argue for your limitations. If you have done something that you regret, then forgive yourself. If you have suffered a loss, then be grateful for the time that person was in your life and move on. Make peace with where you are right now. You cannot change the past, but you can change the way you think about the past. Let bygones be bygones – they are only your reality to the extent that you let them be your reality. The past only needs to take up as much space on your hard disk as you allow it to. It is you and only you who decides how much space it should take up. If your past is painful, then throw it overboard by not focusing on it. You can always choose something else to focus on. You have millions of thoughts to choose from, so why choose thoughts that bring you unhappiness or pain?

The life circumstances that you are living in today are a result of the thoughts you thought in the past. If you want to change anything, then new thoughts are required.

You don't change focus and vibration and consequently point of attraction by going on digging in old wounds. Digging in old wounds holds you in the same old vibration of being the victim and keeps you locked in the sad feeling of then. It is quite inappropriate to send your energy down to old wounds from the past – you cannot change the past, but you yourself can choose how much of your mental space the past should take up now and in the future. It is a choice – and a choice that only you can make. You and you alone are the sovereign master of your thought sphere. If you have not already placed yourself on the ruler's throne, then now may be the time to do it. And when you have taken possession of the throne, then you never have to be influenced by old injuries and the wounds of the past.

Then you can always choose thoughts that are pleasant, and you have the world's best built-in mechanism that tells you which thoughts are good: your emotional guidance system. If a certain thought makes you feel bad, then your emotional guidance system has spoken: Keep away from that thought and choose one that feels better. Always reach out for happy thoughts. Always choose thoughts that feel pleasant. With practice you can reach the point when you never again have to think thoughts that make you sad. When you have reached that point, you have become the master of your mental sphere and of your life.

Tending to Your Vibration

When you are the master of your thoughts, you are also the master of your vibration and of your mental state. When you actively decide to always reach out for happy thoughts, you have taken away the possibility that others could hurt you or make you sad. Other people only have as much power in your thought sphere as you allow them to have. You can practice finding the vibration that releases you from being influenced by the opinion of others, the manipulation of others, their judgment, criticism and the wounds of the past. When you have found the vibration that puts your own emotional wellbeing first, you are free. You are free because you know that the opinion of others is not the final truth about you. Only you have that truth. And when you tend to your own vibration and all the time seek to make the needle of your mental barometer point to happiness, then the opinions of others will be of no consequence to you. Then you can just shrug at their judgment, because it tells nothing about you, it only tells something about them and reveals where they have their thoughts and their own vibration.

Abraham says that the most important thing is to give tender loving care to your own vibration. Pay attention to where you have your own vibration, and if it has sunk below zero, then quickly reach out for thoughts that can bring it back above zero. Don't be indifferent to feeling low. It is very important to keep your vibration high, so that the needle points to happiness and "joi de vivre" because then everything else follows suit: health, contentment, abundance, fun, love, happiness and joy.

When you master the art of changing focus, so that the barometer always points to happiness, then you have taken possession of a very powerful tool, because then you have taken the reins of your own life. And when you concentrate on happy thoughts and on visualizing a happy and glorious future, then you will very soon see and feel the improvements in your life. The improvements and the "tailwind" will be guaranteed as soon as you, through a change in your focus, change your vibration and consequently your point of attraction, because the law of attraction will see to it. Contentment attracts more contentment, abundance attracts more abundance, health attracts better health, love attracts more love etc. And, as Abraham says again and again: *"Life is supposed to be fun".* We are meant to be happy. And when we are meant to be happy, it is because it is of importance to the whole.

Our Individual Thoughts Are Important to the Whole

It is of importance which type of thoughts each and every one of us thinks, because our thoughts affect the whole of the spiritual atmosphere of the Earth. The happier we are, the more we lift the spiritual atmosphere of the Earth towards the light. On this subject Martinus says:

"You often hear that people think that it is of no importance what the individual human being thinks, says and does on a daily basis, and that it is only the "big and strong" who have influence. But that is not true. Anyway it depends on what you mean by "big and strong". Every single human being and his longings and wishes are important to the whole. I have said earlier that the Earth is a living being in whose physical organism the whole humanity constitutes the organ that can be compared to the brain in our own organism. The individual human beings constitute a kind of brain cells in the physical organism of the Earth, and it is of great importance to the whole which energy vibrations are emitted from the individual parts of the whole." (Martinus: "Longing", Kosmos 2, 2003, my underlining added).

With our thoughts we affect the joint thought climate of the Earth, and the more we can "lift" our thoughts towards happiness, gratitude, enthusiasm, joy, humanity and universal love, the more we affect the whole positively. Worry, self pity, pessimism and dooms-day thoughts do not help the whole or lift it towards the light.

Abraham agrees that all kinds of worry and pessimism are completely misplaced and unnecessary. Abraham points out that life on Earth has never been better: a larger part of the population of the Earth is better off today than ever before. The Earth is a wonderful place to live and experience contrast, and it is not, as many people seem to think these days, moving towards destruction, over population and doom.

When so many of us today believe that the planet is on the verge of destruction, it is because it is always the negative aspects that are in focus. The focus is on terrorism, war, pollution, lack, climate change, earth quakes, starvation etc. The focus is never on the enormous technological advances that many of us are benefiting from and the improved conditions of life that a large part of the population of the planet lives under today. Imagine, if the news would focus on the abundance that many of us live in, the beautiful and pleasant houses many of us live in, the prosperity we live in (the Danes have doubled their riches since the 1970s), the selection of consumer goods we can choose from, the thousands of new ways in which we can fill our stomachs, the huge selection that is on offer for our entertainment via television, radio, movies, theatres, operas etc., the ease with which we communicate via e-mail and mobile phones, the enormous advantage we have of the Internet when it comes to seeking information, the ease with which we can travel around the world, our improved ability to cure illnesses (today we can cure a whole number of illnesses that were incurable only a few decades ago), our prolonged life expectancy, and the physical health that many, who only a few decades ago were considered "old", are enjoying today. Millions of people have a much better life than they had only one generation ago and live in conditions that our parents could only dream about. The positive aspects outbalance the negative ones to a large extent, but there is rarely any focus on them. A person who has the ability to focus (we all have) can choose freely between focusing on the positive aspects instead of the negative. And by doing that, he or she can help lift the joint vibration of the Earth for the benefit of the whole.

Everything on the planet is under control by forces that are far stronger than us, because the Earth is, as already mentioned, a living being. Also the number of individuals that have reincarnated here, is regulated by the Earth "I". Abraham points out that the planet has room for a far larger population than it has today and that there is absolutely nothing wrong with the conditions here. *"Your world is not broken"* says Abraham again and again.

When many peoples' thoughts run along the same lines, this stream of thought becomes a considerable factor in the joint thought climate of the Earth. Today we have thought trends that focus on terrorism, global warming, pollution and over-population. Abraham often underlines that being against something is not appropriate, because by focusing on what you are against, you attract it. Instead of being against terrorism, against pollution, against war, against hunger, against global warming, it would be much better to be for peace, for abundance for everybody, for pure and sustainable sources of energy, for global harmony etc. When you are for something, you attract what you are for, but when you are against something, you also attract what you are against, because in an attraction-based universe, you attract what you focus on, even if it is something unwanted. It is much better for the whole, if you concentrate on visualizing what you want, instead of focusing on what you don't want.

To Focus on What Is

If you only focus on what you can observe "out there" that is what you attract. Many people have completely stopped wishing for anything and they only relate to what they can observe in the world. They watch the news on television and this news becomes, together with what they observe in their surroundings, their reality. In this way they have created a model of the world that corresponds to what comes in from their senses. That is how it is, they say – that is reality. And they let this perception of the world limit the possibilities of their own lives. They say: it is impossible to get a job, because there is unemployment, it is impossible to get a flat, because there is housing shortage, it is impossible to be cured, because there are waiting lists at the hospitals, it is impossible to have peace, because there is terrorism, it is impossible to have a happy future, because there is global warming etc. They have what Abraham lovingly calls: "whatisitis".

When you focus on "what is", you can only attract "what is". When you beat the drum of "what is" you are keeping yourself apart from that which is in the process of becoming reality based on your wishes. When you focus on unemployment and think: I'll never get a job, because there is unemployment, then you attract more unemployment. In order to attract the opposite, you must focus on the opposite and think: it is easy to get a job, jobs are hanging on the trees – all I have to do is choose which tree to pick from. By focusing on abundance, you attract abundance and by focusing on lack, you attract lack.

If you are used to focusing on what is and want to have changes in your life, then it is useful to remember that you cannot remain in the same place vibrationally and at the same time make changes happen. If you want changes to happen, you must change your thoughts, point of focus and point of view, so that you can change your vibration and consequently your attraction. More of the same will invariably only bring more of the same.

If you want to get out of the tread mill that dictates that the world is in a specific way, defined by everybody else, well, then you should start thinking and wishing beyond what is immediately observable. You should give your thoughts wings and you vision space. You should set your wishes free and feel the fresh, free wings of positive expectations. You should ask yourself what you want more than anything in your life and then focus on it. In other words you should think big, because as somebody said: *"When you are thinking anyway, you might as well think big"*.

To Think Big

Many people have never dared think about their wildest wishes or their fulfillment, quite simply because they did not believe that they would or could come true. They have not been able to see how the wishes could come true, so they have "made do" with smaller wishes, which they thought were more realizable. But there are no limits to the wishes we can have fulfilled. All we need to do is dare to think big, simply to wish that our wildest dreams come true.

If we look around in the world, there are loads of examples of people who have dared think big and have had their wildest dreams come true.

From he was 10 years old Björn Borg dreamt about winning the Wimbledon title. He was the first person to win it 5 years running. From when she was young Kate Moss dreamt about becoming a supermodel. Her teachers at school made fun of her and said that she should be happy, if she could get a job as a cashier in the local supermarket. But Kate stuck with her dream and became a very highly paid supermodel. Jerry Hall (who later married Mick Jagger) was born in Texas in a poor family with 5 children. Her father was an alcoholic and her childhood was marked by fear of the father. But Jerry had a dream. She had a dream of becoming a model and she imagined that she "just" had to go to the French Riviera, walk along the beach in her bikini and then she would be "discovered". With this clear image in her mind, she packed her few belongings in a suitcase and went to the Riviera, only 16 years old. She put on her pink bikini and walked around on the beach. In less than half an hour (!!!), a man turned up who offered her a job as a model. She immediately went to Paris and soon she was on the front page of all fashion magazines. That was the beginning of the career that made her both rich and famous. Just as she had dreamt and visualized.

The list of wild dreams that have come true is miles long and we only have to think about all those who are rich and famous today to see examples of dreams coming true. And one thing is certain: without having dreamt the dream, it cannot come true. If you only dream small, average dreams, well, then it is small, average dreams that come true. You cannot manifest anything that you haven't first visualized or wished.

Visualizing

When you can see the fulfillment of your wish in your mind's eye through visualization, then you are well on your way to having your wish come true. Visualizing is an extremely efficient instrument in the service of the fulfillment of your wishes. If it is health you wish, you should visualize yourself as healthy, cured, well and fit. If it is wealth you wish, you should visualize yourself in the surroundings and with the bank account you want. If it is a boyfriend you wish, then you should see him before you in all his glory. If it is a certain job you wish, you should see yourself as one who is already carrying it out. If it is success within a certain field that you want, you should see yourself in a specific situation, where the success is a reality ...maybe you can already hear the applause. There is no doubt that visualization works.

You can help your visualization along by making a "vision board" with photos or drawings of the realization of your wishes. If you, on a daily basis, see a photo or a drawing of what you want to happen, then you activate the energy in your consciousness and thus you attract it. When you can see it in your mind's eye and see it every day with expectant happiness, then it cannot help manifesting.

Never Worry about the "How"

It is quite possible that many people abstain from wishing big because they cannot imagine how their wish could come true. They think: I cannot become a millionaire, because how could that happen? But the thing is that you don't have to know how your wishes can come true. "The how" is the domain or "problem" of the universe and not something that you should worry about. It can probably help, if you take appropriate steps in the desired direction and let your actions reflect your goal, but an actual knowledge about how your wishes will come true is not necessary. The law of attraction will take care of that, and it means that you have the strongest law in the universe working for the realization of your wishes. When I walked the Camino I had no idea how I could get into the fancy hotel or how I could get bread for lunch, but that was of no importance, because the universe took care of that. My wishes were fulfilled just because I had thought them.

So if you want to become a millionaire, the first thing to do is to check your relationship with money. If your relationship with money is characterized by thoughts of lack, well, then you won't become a millionaire until you have changed your thought pattern. Many people have grown up with the idea that says: You must work hard for your money, there is too little money in the world, it is hard to get enough money, money doesn't grow on trees, there is never enough money, I can't afford this and that, I want to go on holiday, but I can't afford it, I'll never get out of debt, I'll always be poor etc. With these thoughts of lack you are stuck in a poverty consciousness that will keep you in poverty the rest of your life, simply because these thoughts attract more poverty.

In order to get out of your possible poverty consciousness you must change your thought pattern from focusing on lack to focusing on abundance, lots of money and wealth. Instead of thinking as just mentioned, you should think: there is enough of everything, money and riches are flowing everywhere, so they can also flow to me, abundance characterizes the processes of nature (just look at what a single corn of maize can become), the rich attract more and more riches, we live in a universe characterized by abundance, there is lots of everything no matter where you turn. In order to enhance your attraction power you could try practicing some of the affirmations at the end of this book.

As soon as you have changed your thought pattern to being on vibrational wavelength with abundance and riches, then you have opened up the "gate" through which riches and abundance can flow to you. This is something that all really rich people know. Only by thinking abundance and wealth can you attract it.

The Creation of Fate

It should be clear by now that we create our fate and our reality, indeed all the circumstances of our lives, through what we think, focus on and consequently attract. Only we are responsible for our lives. It is no use that we go around blaming others and think it is somebody else's fault if our life does not enfold the way we want it to. Nor is it any use believing that our life is governed by chance. In this attraction based universe nothing happens by chance – everything is governed by natural laws that determine where even the smallest speck of dust lands.

Our fate is in our own hands – nobody else can make decisions about our life. Martinus goes as far as calling our control over our own fate *"[our] own all-important divine power"*.

"The law of attraction and repulsion determines that every individual constantly has the strings of his own fate in his hand and can work incessantly on his own divinity. The most important point for the same individual will be to come to realize or to reach full clarity of his own all-important divine power in

order to use it in the control of his own fate towards the highest peaks". (Martinus: The Ideal Food, booklet 5, chapter 9).

It cannot be pointed our strongly enough that we ourselves have the strings of our fate in our own hands. When, on the other hand, many people think that it is "the others" that control their lives, it is because they still haven't taken a firm hold of the reins and have *"come to realize or to reach full clarity of their own all-important divine power"*. Nobody but you can attract in your life. It is only your own point of attraction, based on your own vibration that works in your life. Your wife, husband, mother, father, brother, sister, daughter, son etc. cannot attract anything in your life. Only you can attract in your life. You only have one factor that attracts and that is your own vibration. And consequently your life is your own responsibility.

If you think that it is your wife, your husband or your mother that runs your life, well, then it is because you let them. And you let them by accepting their arguments, plans or orders and by letting their way of thinking become your own way of thinking and by including it in your vibration, and consequently making it your own point of attraction. But as you are here on the physical plane in order to experience and create according to your own wishes, longings and desires, it is to "pursue a wrong policy" to let others decide over your life. That was not what you came here for.

It is more difficult to keep your own course, based on the direction your own wishes point out, if you are constantly under the influence of external factors or the opinions of others. If you constantly change direction in order to please others, your own course will easily become one of zigzag. If your own wish is to go to Bristol, while your mother thinks it would be better if you went to Manchester, and you let your mother's opinion influence your own course, well then the result will inevitably be a course that zigzags between Bristol and Manchester. And in that way you will never arrive at neither Bristol nor Manchester.

It is not unusual that you are confronted with the demand from others that you should make them happy, that you must not make them sad etc. In that connection it can be useful to understand that you cannot in reality please other people with your behavior for more than a very short time, because you cannot live their lives and you are not responsible for their satisfaction with life. Only they are. It is not your job to make other people happy. It is their own job – they themselves are responsible for their own happiness just as you are responsible for yours. As happiness is the result of a specific choice of thoughts, and consequently of a specific vibration, it is obvious that only you can be responsible for your own satisfaction with life. As impossible it is to think other people's thoughts, as impossible is it to vibrate in the vibration of others. And consequently it is your own business and responsibility to be happy and content. Like so many other things it is your own choice.

People, who insist that others should behave in a certain way, so that they can be happy, are, according to Abraham, far, far out. They are, because no other person can, over a length of time, maintain another person in happiness. Even if he did a belly dance and stood on his head for seven days on end he could not maintain the other person in happiness. To want somebody else to behave in a certain way, is to seek control over others. People, who seek control over others, maintain the other in an unpleasant situation, where he constantly feels that there is something he should do to make the control seeker happy. And then, when he does what he thinks works, then it doesn't work anyway, because then the control seeker will try to gain even more control by demanding that another belly dance be performed by the "victim". One zigs when the other zags and in that way nobody gets happy. Also the control seeker retains himself in a locked situation, because he mistakenly believes that others have to behave in a certain way, so that he can be happy. But you cannot find lasting happiness outside yourself. Only you can find happiness in your life via your choice of focus, and you are the only one responsible for the satisfaction you experience. All attempts of control over others will inevitably fail.

To say the least, Abraham is not impressed with people who seek control over others and try to make their decisions. To a question from a grown man, whose mother still tried to dominate him by telling him that she would be sad, if he didn't do this or that, Abraham said: *"Tell her that she is in deep trouble and that you are not her solution"*. In other words the plea from Abraham to all those who want to control others is: "GET A LIFE" and don't try to control what others do. It is only your own life and your own satisfaction with it that you should seek to get control over – not that of others.

It can be said that you only have full control of your own life when the opinions of others (including those of your mother) are without importance to you. Or said in another way: When the voice and the vision on the inside become more profound, loud and clear than the opinions on the outside, you've mastered your life.

To master your life you were born with an infallible instrument of guidance: your emotional guidance system. If you listen to it, it will give you unerring guidance about what to accept and what not to accept. If something feels good, you can say yes to it, and if it feels bad, you can choose to say no.

Abraham points out that everything you have in your life right now is a result of the thoughts you have thought up until now. Those thoughts have literally invited the circumstances that you are now living under into your life, and the same thoughts have established you in your job, your marriage or partnership, in your house or flat etc. The circumstances of your life are a direct result of what you have thought and consequently attracted up until today.

Your point of attraction is now. It is in the now that you attract what is to come to you later. It is in the now that you attract your future. So if you want to change the circumstances of your life, well, then it is _now_ you must change your attraction. And you change your attraction by focusing on what you want. With your focusing you affect your vibration and with your vibration, you attract. The more you focus on what you want and the more you look forward to its coming with joy and anticipation, the more strength your attraction has. And remember: the more enthusiasm you can convey with your wishes, the faster they will materialize in your life. Happiness, joy, enthusiasm and gratitude are good catalysts for the realization of your wishes.

The Right Attitude

What is the best attitude to have to life? Let us have a look at what Martinus and Abraham have to say about that.

It is of fundamental importance that you accept the responsibility for your life. There is nobody else to blame or praise. Via your thinking and focusing, you have decided where you are today, and you are the one who decides where your life should go. Happy thoughts, focusing on joy and gratitude are infallibly the road to a light and happy fate.

"Man's road out of suffering is this to practice an optimistic and humanistic way of thinking. Without this way of thinking there is no perfect life force in the human organism and mentality. But the human being himself must help set his life force straight. Just as the gardener must weed the areas where he grows fruit, so that the trees are not suffocated by weeds, so must Man also weed his consciousness, his terrain for the cultivation of his thoughts and the conduct of his will, to remove the suffocating weeds that can flourish here and have a debilitating and paralyzing effect on its life force and normality and thus destroy his zest for life or happiness at being alive. This mental weeding consists in removing pessimism and all bitterness towards beings that you think are the authors of your sufferings or trouble. This becomes easier when you remove all sense of martyrdom and self pity and all complaints about your state of affairs towards other beings and understand that life from a cosmic point of view is just and perfect and that you yourself is responsible for your fate ...

Positive life force arises from optimistic thought forms, you see. If, on the other hand, the thought forms of a being are based on pessimism and doomsday thoughts, self pity and a sense of martyrdom and bitterness towards other people, whom he thinks are the cause of his sufferings, these will only produce negative, meso cosmic electrical impulses and consequently a very *deficient or debilitated life force. But a debilitated life force means debilitated functioning of both organism and mentality. Such a debilitated function can again only give birth to a weakened zest for life or joy of being alive. To feel joy of life and happiness to be alive is a function. But functions can only be conveyed by force. To the same degree that the force is lacking, the function stops. These debilitations of force are the real cause of all existing mental and bodily illnesses. And these can even bring the being to commit suicide, which is the same as the culmination of foolishness. The inner cause of all illnesses is thus erroneous thinking and perception. The being must stake everything on achieving optimistic thoughts, which can be achieved by realizing the essential truth of life, which in itself is the culmination of optimism, based in its identity with universal love."* (Martinus: "Answer to a letter from a sick man", Kosmos 5, 2007)

When you think positive thoughts, you get positive life force. With positive life force you magnetize your blood positively and thus you create both physical and spiritual health. As your fate is your own responsibility, it is no use reproaching others for your present situation. The realization of your own 100 % responsibility for your fate and a weeding out in your mentality of bitter and black thought forms is the road forward towards happiness and good health, says Martinus.

Abraham couldn't agree more. If all you get out of the teachings of Abraham is that you should reach out for happiness, then Abraham is happy, because then you have understood the main message: "you're good, be happy". With happy thoughts you attract all that is positive: good health, prosperity, satisfaction and the realization of your wishes. If you would only concentrate on your "emotional journey" towards always feeling happy and give up all sorts of negativity and "resistance", then both health and the realization of your wishes will follow suit. Because, when you transmit happiness, you are a strong attractor and consequently your wishes will come true quickly and effortlessly. Abraham goes as far as saying that every negative thought is a step in the direction of something unwanted materializing in your life. With prolonged insisting on negative, sad, bitter and "it is not my fault" thoughts, you are surely and irrevocably moving towards the materialization in your life of illness, accidents and unwanted circumstances. According to Abraham every ornery moment is a step on the road towards something unwanted manifesting in your life. It is easier to turn the boat around before the unwanted manifests, and you turn the boat by steering away from bad, negative and unhappy thoughts. Through letting go of bad thoughts, you can reach out for mental freedom, so that you achieve a sense of relief. With relief you can reach out for happier and even happier thoughts, and thus you can move away from all the unwanted. You can say to yourself: *"I'm going to look for the best feeling thought I have access to".* In that way you can move up the emotional scale. That is the essence of the emotional journey and as you move up the scale by reaching out for better and better feeling thoughts, you are well on the way to achieving the right attitude, whose basis is gratitude, appreciation, happiness and joy.

Psyche and Soma

When you actively work to improve your emotional state, then an improved bodily state will inevitably follow suit. Psyche and soma are so closely related that only a small mental improvement in the direction of happiness, relief and wellbeing will immediately lead to more bodily health. Abraham says that feeling happiness and wellbeing is *".. the fountain of youth, the river of wellness, the stream of abundance, the way to all things that are important to you".*

Abraham also says: *"You could have every deadly disease known to man in your body right now and we could promise you that if you could guide your thoughts toward better and better feeling things, you would move away from the resistance that is the disallowing factor of the wellness."*

It is the disallowing of wellbeing that creates illness, so to the extent that wellbeing is lacking in your life, you are attracting illnesses and undesired things.

There seems to be a tendency to get too hung up for too long on things that are bothering you. Let it go! And don't be unconscious about your thoughts and feelings; be conscious about how you are feeling. Keep a constant check on how you are feeling, because negative emotions always mean that you are moving towards something that you'll not like, when you get there. The thing is that people look at and think about things they do not want, they ignore their emotional guidance system, and then when the unwanted things turn up in their life, they say: where did that come from? Seek to always feel good - in that way you will not attract the unwanted. The way you feel is a choice, because there are other feelings and other frequencies available. Reach out for the vibration that frees you of the bind.

If, for a long time, you have had dark thoughts, and an illness has now manifested in your life in response to the negative attraction you have effected, well, then you can move away from the illness again by moving up the emotional scale by reaching out for happier feelings. And to the extent that you can move up the emotional scale towards thoughts of happiness, to the same extent will the illness subside. Every step towards more happiness and joy is a step towards bodily health. And relief from dark thoughts and pessimism is the best possible cure. Abraham says: *"Relief is the cure that all medicine is looking for".*

Abraham says that if you have had a serious diagnosis, it is important that you concentrate on a hope of getting well. The vibration in hope is a healing vibration as opposed to the vibration in fear and powerlessness, which pulls you in the opposite direction. Again it is of paramount importance that you, also in a situation where an illness has manifested, take responsibility for your own cure. By thinking hope and optimism you are moving up the scale towards health. Putting your life and health totally in the hands of doctors is quite inappropriate. It is not the doctor who has attracted your illness. Only you can attract in your life. If you have attracted the illness, you can push it away again by thinking and attracting good health, hope, cure and happiness. Nobody else can do that but you.

All diseases are responses to a sustained vibrational pattern that you have been offering, and, according to Abraham, the vibrational illness-equivalent to various vibrational patters would be: To overwhelment or frustration the illness- equivalent would be: headaches, muscle aches, cramps. To self-awareness, self-consciousness, self-criticism, "I want to look good, I fear I don't" the equivalent would be: A hairy mole on your face. To anger and rage the equivalent would be strokes and heart diseases. To despair, fear, lack of control, and if there is something in your life that is really bothering you, the equivalent would be something that replicates your feeling of powerlessness, and that could be something serious like cancer.

So, if an illness has manifested, then change frequency – there are other frequencies available than the ones that are responsible for the illness. When you work on an improved emotional condition, then your vibration changes and the bodily condition must follow. So try to find a way to feel a little better right now. The better you feel the more health you will attract. Just choose to feel better – you don't have to change any circumstances. In cases of illness, the most important thing you can do is to improve your emotions and consequently your vibration. Your work is your emotional journey. Your aim is to "be there" vibrationally. The higher and happier your vibration, the better your health.

Follow Your Bliss

Make sure that you don't attract "by default" by letting chance decide where you have your thoughts and consequently your vibration and your point of attraction. If you are just letting yourself be dragged around the ring of the circus of life according to how the wind blows, it can easily happen that you attract circumstances in your life that you actually don't want. Also in this area of life it is important to pay careful attention. Take care of your vibration, be aware where you have your thoughts, mind your mental climate, let it be important to you how you feel, take responsibility for your own satisfaction and make sure that you are happy. Make it the biggest project of your life to be happy. Then everything else follows.

Accept that you are not perfect (nobody is). Make peace with where you are and be easy on yourself. Just be happy to be alive.

"Follow your bliss", Abraham says again and again. Go where your wishes take you. When you do that, you are constantly working on the realization of your happiness, and with joy and positive expectation you attract all the things you want in your life. As Abraham puts it: *"If you were following your bliss, you would be tuned in, tapped in, turned on."*

Is It Egoism?

Now, there might be somebody who is of the opinion that focusing on the fulfillment of your own wishes is egoism. Abraham readily accepts that it can be called egoism to a certain extent. But the world has been constructed in such a way that you can only attract in your own vibration, and that means that you can only attract according to your own wishes and desires. It is only your own vibration that you have control of. You cannot attract in anybody's vibration but your own.

But that doesn't mean that you cannot help others. And it must be underlined that it is particularly when you have obtained the fulfillment of your own wishes that you can be of benefit to others. It is on the basis of your own abundance and the surplus energy from your own self realization that you find resources to help others. You can hardly help others when you yourself are in lack, are dissatisfied, unhappy or down on your luck. Therefore: what is best for you, is also best for others and consequently for the whole. And it is a well-known fact that the largest contributors to charity and aid projects of the planet are those who have had success themselves and can give freely from their resources.

Martinus looks at the question of the fulfillment of our wishes and desires in the largest of perspectives. Without wishes and desires there would be no future for Mankind, because it is with our wishes that we shape the future.

"... likewise there would be no future for Mankind if their consciousness wasn't filled with wishes and longings." (Martinus: "Longings", Kosmos 2, 2003).

On our eternal journey our wishes and desires are our compass telling us which course to take. What else could tell us which way to go, if it wasn't our own desires? Which other factor could mark our course? Martinus points out that the meaning of life is to experience it. Because it is through experience of life and experience of contrast that we renew our consciousness. And because we are cells in the giant body that we can call the Source or God, our experience of life is important to the whole. Because it is through us that the

Godhead experiences life. As already mentioned "he" has no external experience of life and can consequently only experience it via us, his micro cosmos. The experience of life is of paramount importance to the renewal of consciousness on both micro- and macro cosmic levels. And the fulfillment of our own wishes marks the peaks of experience on our route through eternity.

As our wishes are our personal compass on our eternal journey, and as our wishes are fundamental for the creation of the society of the future it can hardly be said to be egoistic to have our wishes fulfilled.

But on the other hand Martinus makes it clear that wishes that in the short or long run are not beneficial to the whole will be corrected through life's own speech. Life's own speech expresses itself via the consequences that our choice of wishes has for our destiny. The point is to learn to wish "the right thing". And what then, is the "right thing"? It is wishes that are beneficial to the whole.

To Wish "The Right Thing"

We will all be good at wishing "the right thing" when sometime in the future we become all-loving beings without traces of animal mentality. But today we are all, to a larger or lesser degree, marked by mental traces of our animal past. It is these animal traces in our psyche that make us able to boast, hurt, cheat, lie, hate, steal, feel envy or jealousy, have outbursts of anger and carry out murder and killings. Today we are somewhere between being animal and human. We are, with Martinus' words, unfinished human beings, or *"wounded fugitives between two kingdoms"*, the animal kingdom and the real human kingdom. To the same degree that the animal mentality is rooted in our psyche, we will wish egoistically, and to the same degree that the human mentality is rooted, we will wish the right thing. Wishing the right thing is something we must learn.

"It is natural for the animal in earthly Man suddenly to emit thoughts of anger or revenge and wish something unpleasant for another human being, but it is not natural for the human being in earthly Man. The earthly human beings have no real control over their wishes; they are practically illiterates in the area of wishes. But does it matter at all what one wishes? Indeed it does. The entire present situation of Man is a result of Man's, from a human perspective, unnatural wishes. Wishes create destiny. In the future wishing will be a subject in school, so that we can learn to get control of our ability to wish. It is of absolutely vital importance to all cultural creation to fight the unnatural wishes. There will be no peace in the human state until there is peace in the human mind, and there will be no peace in the human mind until Man has learnt to wish as a human being and not as an intellectual predator." (Martinus: "When you play hazard with life", Kosmos 11, 2000, Martinus' underlining).

The human beings of today are close to being illiterates in the area of wishing, says Martinus. They are illiterates because they think that their wishes are of no importance to their lives and to the whole. But that is not so, because wishes create fate. For that reason it is of paramount importance that we realize that our wishes will come true, and that we constantly ask ourselves if we are wishing like humans or like intellectual predators. Today we see the consequences of the wishes of the intellectual predators of power, revenge, blood thirst and riches at the cost of everybody else in all those places where there is unrest, war, terrorism, thirst for revenge and accidents. These wishes are, from a human point of view, unnatural and do not match the human side of the human being. It is of vital importance to our creation of culture to fight the unnatural wishes. For that reason we will, in the society of the future, be taught how to wish "the right thing", i.e. to wish something that benefits the whole.

But, of course, we can distinguish between wishes that are detrimental to the whole, where, for instance, somebody usurps things or advantages at the cost of his neighbor, and more innocent wishes, which do no harm to anybody and which respect everybody's right to live. Among the more innocent wishes we find: achieving a specific job, finding the right life companion, living in a certain place, having one's needs for food, shelter and entertainment satisfied, being well and healthy all through life etc. Even if these wishes can, to a certain extent, be said to be egoistic, as they are all about the self realization of the "I", they can hardly be said to be detrimental to the whole.

And then there is the point about "loving your neighbor as yourself". You should love your neighbor, but also love yourself. And an important part of loving yourself is to have your fundamental needs covered together with the wishes that give the soul wings and consequently help raise the joint vibration of the Earth. It is also through the fulfillment of our wishes that we become satiated in a certain field of experience and consequently can get hungry in a new field. Hunger and satiation are the driving forces in all creation of experience. The creation of experience is fundamental to our development, and our wishes mark the course of development. Without wishes, no course.

We Can Choose Freely from All Shelves

All our wishes must be fulfilled, because only then can the cycle of the wish be concluded. And in this all-loving universe it is so that there is not a single experience that we, the quanta of God, are not allowed to experience. All possible experiences, all sorts of likely and unlikely creations are allowed. If there were just the slightest limitation in what we were allowed to experience, our creation of experience could not become complete. We really can choose whatever we like from all the shelves of the supermarket.

In our past we have had animal wishes that we have had fulfilled. And what are the consequences of the fulfillment of the animal wishes? What are the consequences of having maimed, killed, executed, waged war and all the other so-called evil? Why are we even allowed to carry out all those bad acts? Let us have a look at this interesting question.

"The divine "something" or the "I" behind the organism is thus... completely free with respect to all energies or types of matter in life. Any energy obeys the least of its wishes or commands. And it is as a response to this command or wish that their present organism and consciousness, indeed their whole fate, have been created. Every detail, both the microscopic ones and the more visible ones in this fate, is unmistakably the fulfillment of former wishes and desires with respect to the choice of the energies or types of matter relevant to fate. Should the chosen energies at a later point in time prove not to be able to harmonize, and created an unhappy fate, then this can only give the "I" experiences. And as it is immortal in its nature, and consequently can survive all mistakes and choose again, it can, on the strength of these experiences, in the future avoid choosing the same wrong energies. That it can thus choose unwisely shows, as already mentioned, a one hundred percent freedom for the "I" or the living "something" in the beings. It has total freedom with respect to the types of matter and can thus, according to its nature, wishes and desires, express or influence its creation, its manifestation and appearance in nuances that go from the culmination of harmony to the culmination of disharmony. The "I" can thus make use of whatever type of matter it may wish in its creation, but it must come to understand that the types of matter follow their mission. They do not change character in order to correct the mistakes of the "I". (Martinus: LB II, paragraph 307, my underling added).

All energies and consequently all types of matter are at the free disposal of the "I" in its accumulation of experience. The "I", or the living "something" in every physical organism, can choose freely among all thinkable manifestations, spanning from those that create harmony to those that create disharmony. Everything is thus allowed, and you never run out of time to carry it out in. Eternity is your playground and all types of matter obey your will. And because there are oceans of time, it is no problem that you make mistakes, choose unwisely and mix the energies in an inappropriate way. You can just redo it. Your "I" survives all the mistakes, the mistakes are stored in your fate element as experience and this means that the next time, you will choose more wisely and in the end get it just right.

That again means that there is no need to worry if you, in a specific incarnation, don't get it all done quite right. Let us say that you, in this life, haven't achieved everything you wanted, maybe you behaved badly, you went to prison, you got in with a bad crowd, you let somebody down, you stole, you persecuted somebody etc. Seen in a one life perspective such a destiny is unfortunate and sad, indeed somebody might even call it "wasted", but seen in the perspective of eternity, it is just a small ripple on the sea, a small stone on the road, a "wrong" grasp in the bag with the energies. There is lots of time to get it better, to redo things, to repair the damage. Seen in the perspective of eternity there are no failures, no tragedies, no irreparable damage. There is only accumulation of experience, tasting of the adventure of life and renewal of consciousness through the experience of contrast. What you didn't get right in this incarnation, you can do better in the next, and in the next, and in the next... And your possible mistakes and "wrong grasp" in the bag with the energies don't make you a less worthy being, don't make you a sinner in the eyes of God and don't send you down to eternal flames. Because all living beings are quanta of God or "extensions of source energy" all are worthy and important to the whole. Nobody is unworthy, lost or "forgotten" by God.

Just as there are no limitations in your availability of time and energies, there are no limitations in your possibilities for creation of experience. You are allowed to lie, cheat, steal, hurt, kill and execute. No angel will jump out of the closet to prevent you from committing adultery, and there is no fiery writing across the sky, when you are about to commit a murder. You are free to do those things. The types of matter follow their mission and do not change character in order to prevent you from committing a bad deed. The dagger, which you are about to use for a murder, will not suddenly turn into a bird's feather to prevent the murder from being carried out. If you want to kill, you can go right ahead and do it. If killing is an experience that you want to have in your experience file, then you are free to create this experience. But, but, but.....

We shall look at the "buts" in the next chapter about the law of karma.

7. Karma

In this chapter we shall have a look at the regulating factor, which as its final effect has that we'll all stop lying, cheating, bragging, stealing, killing, murdering, executing and going to war. We'll have a look at the absolutely genial teaching that we are all subject to from the Universe or Providence: the law of karma or "as you sow you shall reap". What we do to others we in effect do to ourselves. If we steal, we will be stolen from, if we lie, we will be lied to, if we cheat, we will be cheated and if we kill, we will be killed. (10).

Our voyage on the physical plane is all about accumulation of experience. Experience creates wisdom. The more lives we live, the more experience we reap, and the more experience we reap, the more humane and loving we become. Development can only go forward in the sense that over the lives and in tune with the reaping of experience and suffering, more and more wisdom is "built into" the beings. It is through the experiences of many, many lives that we become altruistic and all-loving humans through a gradual cleansing of our animal desires. One can say that life itself reads the proofs of "wrong wishes", i.e. wishes that are not to the benefit of the whole. Wishes of revenge, murder, restitution of honor, self-worship, egotism and the like, which are exclusively about self-focused lust for power and of a 100 % egoistic nature, will relentlessly be corrected by life itself.

In the above-mentioned quotation from Martinus it says: "*That the chosen energies at a later point possibly turned out to be in mutual disharmony and created an unhappy fate, can only bring experience to the "I". And as it is immortal in its nature and thus in reality can survive all mistakes and make new choices, it can, via these experiences, in the future avoid choosing the same wrong energies.*"

When with time the "I" learns to avoid the wrong energies, it is because all energies move in cycles. Sooner or later the energy, which for instance caused a killing, will return to its point of departure i.e. to the "I" that caused the killing. And when it does, it means that the "I" will lose the physical body, that it is at present animating, through a murder. In other words, as it itself murdered, it will be murdered. The "I" has sown murder, and will therefore reap murder. It is life's relentless justice that is thus expressed. What we do to others, we eventually do to ourselves.

Our Karma Is also Orchestrated by the Law of Attraction

Again it is the law of attraction that directs the waves of karma. When the energy of a specific act has completed its cycle and has returned to its source, it is "deposited" in the aura of the originator. And once it has been deposited in the aura, it has become a part of the attraction of that individual. He will, for that reason, attract energies that are on wavelength with the specific action of the past.

"As already mentioned any act is a release of karmic or psychic energy, which, after having completed a cyclic movement, returns to its source and there is included in the aura, which then again has the effect that our surroundings or our neighbor will react to us in the same way as we reacted to them." (Martinus: "The Forgiveness of Sins", version 3, Kosmos 1, 2003).

Let us illustrate this with an example. We have an originator of a specific act. For the sake of convenience we call this originator James. Once in the past James has committed an act, whose energy has now returned to its source – to James himself. This means that the energy of the act is now included in the vibration or aura of James. Once it has been included in James' vibration, it means that he now attracts energies on the same wavelength as the act. If the act was a murder, it means that James attracts murder. And that again means that he will, sooner or later, be the victim of murder through the attraction of murderous energies that he is effecting on his surroundings. One day a murderer will come by and kill James. But the murder was "ordered" by James through the act of murder he once committed himself and can, in a cosmic sense, not be blamed on the perpetrator, Charles, who in this case is just an instrument for James' own murderous energies. When Charles is a useful instrument, it is because he also had HIS aura filled with murderous energies that could be attracted by James' murderous energies. Because both James and Charles have "murder on their brains" they can be attracted by each others' energies and the murder "ordered" by James can only be carried out by someone that is on energetic wavelength with the murder, i.e. by another murderer.

A really peace loving person, it could for instance be Mother Teresa, who has no murderous energies in her aura, would by no means be attracted to James' murderous energies, as she has no form of murderous vibration included in her own vibration. For that reason she would be useless as an instrument for James' karma, quite simply because she has no energies in her aura that can be attracted by James' murderous energies. A murderer can only be murdered by another murderer. There has to a match of vibration between the two.

But what when a child is killed or murdered, you may now ask. When a child is killed it is that child's karma that is unfolded. In a former incarnation the child may have caused the death of children or may have sown death and destruction to many people including children. Nothing happens by chance and when somebody, anybody is killed, it is that person's karma. In this connection we should remember that there is no final death and that the karma is "just" the reaping of seeds that the person himself has sown.

The law of karma means that everything that happens to us is an expression of the highest justice. You cannot attract an energy that you yourself have not sent out first, because all energies move in cycles. All acts, that you have carried out, will come back to you as fate or destiny. It happens in the way that the energy of the act is included in your own vibration, which then attracts energies on the same wavelength. Everything that happens to you is the response of the Universe to your own acts. And the Universe tells you: if you sow thistles, it is thistles that you will reap, and if you sow marigolds, it is marigolds that you will reap. You will reap precisely what you have sown, because with the energy you have sent out, you can only attract energies on the same wavelength. The law of attraction sees to that.

The precise response that the Universe offers to our acts is often by Martinus called "life's own speech". It is through the speech of life that we learn. It is through the speech of life that we reap experience. When James has run around killing his fellow men a certain amount of times and in response to these unloving acts has been killed himself a certain amount of times, well, then he will sooner or later have become wiser. The accumulation of experience is unavoidable, and for that reason James will reach a point, where he is sick and tired of killing. Again it is the principle of hunger and satiation in action: what you have done and consequently reaped a certain number of times will eventually satiate you. At a certain point in time James is so fed up with killings that he can no longer carry them out.

But now it is so that James went away to war, and then he was given a machine gun. With his machine gun he mowed hundreds of his adversaries down. This mowing down means that James has a "deficit" on his murder balance. He has simply killed his fellow human beings more times than times he himself has been killed. But now he has become satiated, fed up and sick and tired of war and killings. Then what happens?

The Principle of "The Forgiveness of Sin"

A principle for the forgiveness of sins actually exists and Martinus explains how it works.

"But as the energy wave has to pass a shorter or longer cycle, it can happen to the intellectual human being that he, even after having committed a murder, and before this energy wave returns, bitterly regrets the act of murder to such

an extent that he would never be able to do it again. Then he needs not experience the effects of the act of killing still in circulation. And this new attitude in the mentality or aura means that the returning wave of killing will be dissolved. The energies from the more loving attitude absorb the murderous energies or cancel them out in the aura, and they will then not be able to have effect on the surroundings or provoke one's fellow man to release the act of murder or revenge, which would otherwise have been one's due. In this case we really have a situation where a being has committed an unloving act whose consequences he will not have to experience." (Martinus: "The Forgiveness of Sins", version 3, Kosmos 1, 2003, my underlining added).

Let us return to James, who now, through his accumulation of experience, has become fed up with war and killing and has become a peace loving human being. He is now completely incapable of killing and cannot even eat meat, as he feels that meat is murder. But he still has killed more times than he himself has been killed. Then what happens with the "surplus" murders that James has committed? They are quite simply erased from his account book. And in this way James has, with an old terminology, received forgiveness from his sins. Again this works based on the law of attraction. When James has become fed up with war and killing, the vibration of his aura changes. The change in vibration means that he no longer has any energies in his aura that can attract the murderous energies. When the previously emitted murderous energies return to James' aura, they bump into a closed door. The door is closed because similar energies attract each other and dissimilar energies repel each other. The murderous energies are repelled by the peace and love energies and the *"returning wave of killing will be dissolved".* Thus James has become "debt free" in murder.

For the sake of completeness it should be mentioned that this process towards satiation of war and killings takes many incarnations, and that an act of killing committed in a former incarnation can become our destiny in a later incarnation, as long as we haven't changed our way of thinking and consequently our point of attraction. But when we have truly come to a complete realization that murder is wrong, then we have been released from dark karma in this field.

"Our dark karma in a specific field ceases the moment we understand that the act, which created it, was wrong, was against nature and thus against the divine will, and when the understanding is so profound that it is not mere knowledge, but has become an inability to manifest the act ever again... You see, the repentance is a sign that you have regretted your act. Having regretted it can have come through a realization of having acted wrongly. For that reason the repentance is in fact the same as a fundamental emphasizing that you have reached the real and absolute understanding of your erroneous ways, so that it

is not a mere powerless, theoretical knowledge. It emphasizes that you experience your erroneous ways, not only with the intellect but also with the heart. And it is this way of perceiving that releases Man from darkness". (Martinus: "The Forgiveness of Sin", version 3, Kosmos 1, 2003).

When you, with all your heart, regret having committed an act and realize that you acted wrongly, then your vibration changes and you can no longer attract energies that are on wavelength with the ones you once emitted. And thus your "sins have been forgiven".

The Energies in the Aura Determine the Release of Fate

Although most of us cannot see other peoples' auras, we do, however, sense the energy of the auras. We sense the radiation of other people and in many cases we react to it. The energies are accumulated in the aura, and these energies attract energies that are on the same wavelength. A rowdy man will feel attracted to another rowdy man, whose energy he will perceive as "inviting a fight". The smallest provocation will mean that the two get into a fistfight. "The common denominator" in the aura of the two means that there is a strong attraction, and that again means that the karmas of both can be released.

A peace loving person, however, will not be attracted to the rowdy man, and will not see him as "inviting a fight". The peace loving person will just walk by, and the rowdy man will leave him alone. There is no attraction as there is no similarity in vibration. Even a whole gang of thieves can feel repelled by very loving energies, and consequently they will leave the peace loving person alone.

Martinus was once exposed to an assault by a gang of thieves, and he described it in the book "Martinus – memoirs".

"Is it true that one night you were attacked by some hooligans in Copenhagen?

Yes – in the evening I often took the tram to the centre of the city. I liked to look at the crowds in the streets.

One evening I was walking along Øster Voldgade near the Botanical Garden. It was quite late, and there were no people around. Suddenly 5 guys stepped out from a shrubbery. They assumed a threatening posture, and one of them was just about to punch me in the face with his fist. But the biggest one of them, who appeared to be the "leader of the gang", shouted: "No –don't hit that man".

After that he stepped up to me and said calmly: "We just want your purse and your watch!"

I took the situation with calm and answered: "Unfortunately I don't have a purse on me, but I have this watch, and if you think that you have more right to own it than I have, then you may take it!"

He took the watch and stepped over to the four others. For a moment he was negotiating with them. Then he came back and said: "No – we don't want your watch after all. Now you'll get it back, and then you should just remain standing here until we're gone - and then that's the end of the story!"

Martinus was protected from robbery and assault by his karma and his loving radiation. He explains how this "mechanism" functions in the following quotation:

" ... When a being releases an act, then he emits, via this act, a wave of force shaped according to the act. But as no movement can go in an absolutely straight line, but must always go back to its source, then this psychic wave of force will also go back to its source. Via the act, through which it was sent out, it has attained shape and content. If it is an act of revenge, that was released, it will to a very high degree consist of the energy of gravity, which is an energy that provokes violence, hatred and a desire to kill. When this energy comes back to its source, it will be deposited in the aura of the being and make up a part of it. And the more the being releases this type of manifestation, the more of the returning energies will be deposited in the aura and here they will affect the surrounding beings, who are susceptible to this type of thought energy. These will then in almost every situation "see red" when faced with this being and in the worst case they will release the hatred and the desire to kill, which the being once sent out towards his fellow man in the shape of these energies, against the being itself. If they then resulted in the fellow man being killed, then they will likewise result in their originator being killed. It is this energy form in the aura that causes a being to be, as it were, "inviting a fight". Such a being seems irritating, causes other people to feel antipathy or anger against him without any other visible cause. And the beings, who especially sense the being in question as "inviting a fight", are precisely such beings whose aura is particularly filled with the same type of energy. Consequently these beings are easily provoked to "get into a fight", whereas beings who have long ceased to emit such thoughts, don't have them in their aura. But when they don't have these energies in their aura, they cannot attract other thoughts of the same kind or provoke their surroundings to an explosive behavior towards them. The aura can be so pure and devoid of the energy of gravity that even a real bandit or hooligan will step back and ask for forgiveness in a meek voice. But just as dark and hateful acts cause the surroundings to respond with dark and hateful acts and manifestations towards you, so will your light and loving thoughts and behavior cause light and loving manifestations to come to you from your surroundings, to the extent that you have been able to fill your aura with these thought forms. But the perfect aura will be the one that is filled with universal love, the basic tone of the universe. In all situations, where that is the

predominant energy, it protects the being against darkness". (Martinus: "The Forgiveness of Sin", version 3, Kosmos 1, 2003, my underlining added).

We can put it like this: Just as your own thoughts of murder and revenge attract identical energies and consequently make you susceptible to acts of murder and revenge, so will light and all-loving thoughts make you susceptible to light and love. And with these light and loving thoughts you are protected against dark acts. As we saw in the case of Martinus, his light and loving radiation meant that he was protected against violence and theft. And we can all improve our protection against acts of darkness from our surroundings by improving our mix of thoughts towards being more positive and loving. The more humanitarian and all-loving thoughts our consciousness holds, the higher and purer will our vibration be, and the more are we protected against assaults and acts of violence.

We can also purify our aura by never participating in murder of animals through meat eating. When we eat meat, we are accomplices in the murder of the animal even though we do not kill the animal ourselves. The vibration of the meat will sit in our aura and attract acts of violence or murder. Eating meat is not a good idea if we want to be protected towards accidents or killing.

Today many people think that they can be protected against assault and attacks by owning a gun. If somebody came along with the intention to rob or hurt them, then they could shoot that person and thus be protected. They don´t know that this is no protection at all. Having the intention to shoot and maybe kill another human being if he attacks you is a mix of thoughts that is anything but loving and it will fill the aura with "bad vibes" and thus attract assault. The ONLY protection a person has is his own aura and when it is filled with humanitarian, all-loving thoughts, then we have real protection. There is no other protection.

Karma Is the Pedagogic of Life

Karma is a loving instruction, the greatest teacher and the pedagogic of life. The pedagogic of life is one of consequence, as it is the consequences of our own acts that we are allowed to experience. What we have done to others will inevitably be our own fate. We can say that life itself pays back in kind. And just because our karma will return to us as long as our aura still contains energies that are on wavelength with the energies that we once sent out, it is completely unnecessary to think along the lines of getting revenge for things that somebody has done to us. We don't have to think: "she must pay for this", because what somebody has done to us will be their own karma. Life's own payback is guaranteed - we don't have to lift a finger to ensure that justice be done. If somebody has insulted us, we can just shrug in the certainty that life itself will correct the matter. What a certain person has done to us will be that person's own destiny. The law of attraction will see to it that the person attracts energies that are on wavelength with the insult. Justice will always be done, because that is how the universe is organized.

That again means that our accumulation of experience over many lives sees to it that we all sooner or later will become peace loving human beings who are incapable of killing. Even the terrorist or the suicide bomber will, at a certain point in time, become a peace loving being through the reaping of his own karma. When the suicide bomber has become the victim of suicide bombers or similar acts of violence a certain amount of times, his sufferings will teach him to avoid violence. Because life itself reads the proofs of our acts, the result is given: Through the reaping of experience and sufferings we will all become Man in the image and likeness of God. When enough of us have become that, then a realm of peace will arise on Earth. The result is guaranteed and that is precisely why Martinus can say that "everything is very good". Everything is exactly as it should be on this planet based on our former acts. We are standing right now in the middle of an immense reaping of karma. We still haven't finished reaping.

Martinus compares the present stage of the Earth with the sour stage of an apple. A sour apple is one that is still not ripe or "finished". But with time the apple will become ripe and then it will be a perfect creation. The Earth still hasn't reached the perfect, ripe stage, where everybody lives in harmony with everybody, but the perfect stage is in the process of being created. And it lies beyond doubt that the perfect stage will be reached. The result is a "given" and we can say that war and unrest can be seen as "nothing but" catalysts for the manifestation of the perfect stage.

During a war a lot of people will get their dark karma back at the same time, and in that way they will evolve quickly towards becoming peace loving. People, who have experienced the horrors of war, will, when they are reborn, be against war. Through their experience and satiation of war their vibration will change and consequently their point of attraction. A peace loving person does not attract war and is consequently protected against war by his own vibration.

Karmic Tailwind

The more karma you reap, the more you learn, and the more you reap, the more loving you become. Also your good and loving acts create karma and the more love you sow, the more love you will reap. Martinus has the following to say about the beings that have now reached the point where they are predominantly loving:

"To the same degree that the being is all-loving, nature begins to open its sources. The being not only discovers how many things in its daily life shape

themselves in its favor, without it having staged them. It discovers that it has more and more tailwind in everything it does. And gradually this noticeable tailwind becomes so strong that the being cannot go on believing that it is due to chance. Gradually it begins to be filled with a feeling of gratitude, a desire to thank the invisible forces that are thus more and more obviously in its favor." (Martinus: "The Forgiveness of Sin", version 3, Kosmos 1, 2003)

The more loving you are, the more love you will attract, and the more *"things shape themselves in your favor"*. This means that you will experience more and more tailwind in everything you do. And that is precisely the same as what Abraham says: the more positive and grateful you are, the better you attract. When you are loving, you quite simply attract the things you want and need. Things just come to you, without you knowing how, and often without you being aware of having expressed the wish. Because you are loving, you attract all the energies that you "are lacking" without having staged the delivery. Life complies with your wishes, everything just comes to you, be it abundance, health, friendships and success in everything you do. With such a karmic tailwind you cannot help feeling grateful and consequently:

"One cannot go on expressing the growing feeling of gratitude towards cold, dead, desultory natural forces. The materialist's awakening feeling of gratitude towards Providence is the first awakening of cosmic consciousness. It gradually becomes a living notion that there has to be a living being behind the forces of nature, that there has to be a living, conscious will behind all the events that happen, as they express a logical plan, make up a logical whole. And this notion gradually becomes unshakeable certainty. And one fine day, when the being is especially full of gratitude and love of life, then this certainly enters the awake, physical day consciousness." (Martinus: "The Forgiveness of Sin", version 3, Kosmos 1, 2003).

When things shape themselves in your favor and you experience that you are in contact with higher forces that back you up and respond to your wishes and needs, well, then it becomes more and more impossible to maintain the idea that we live in a godless universe, governed by chance and chaos. Such a perception becomes quite simply impossible. You cannot avoid seeing that there is consciousness, intelligence and logic behind the creations of nature, and you cannot help being grateful that you live in a universe that is governed by laws, and where love is the basic tone. Such a feeling of gratitude will one day lead to your having your first cosmic glimpse. When it happens, you will, through your own day consciousness, experience that you are an immortal being and that the universe is a good and loving place to be. Then you don't need religions, churches, spiritual communities, materialistic science or anything else. Then you no longer need to believe, because you know. Then you have become your own source of wisdom, just as Martinus and Abraham are.

8. Conclusion to Part One

A Powerful Force of Nature and a Powerful Tool

The law of attraction is the strongest natural force in the universe. All matter, be it physical or spiritual (electromagnetic radiation) is subject to the law of attraction, because there is no energy that is not attracted to other energies on the same wavelength.

As we ourselves are energy and as our spiritual body vibrates on a specific wavelength, we attract everything that is on the same wavelength. There is no hocus-pocus about it, because we know that that is how the law of attraction works.

Now that a law of attraction exists and now that this law has a major influence on how our lives enfold, then it seems like high time that we become aware of it and that we start working actively to make this law work for our benefit.

We can make the law work for our own benefit by focusing on and thus attracting what we want to happen. We can begin by getting acquainted with the law and then see how we can make it work for us. Trying is completely free. It takes no major efforts, it takes no special preparations and it doesn't cost anything. And there is not a shadow of a doubt that the law works. And when it works, it also works for you.

You can practice and thus let yourself be convinced about the workings of the law by starting with small things. You can start by attracting a cup of coffee, a parking space, a bird's feather, a meal, a cake, a smile, a kind word, a flower etc. When you see that these things manifest easily in your life, then you can go on to bigger things and circumstances, the perfect partner, the best place to live, the job of your dreams etc. And you attract by focusing on what you want with positive expectation and joy. So, there is only one thing to say: try. All you have to do is try, even though you don't believe in it: it works anyway.

The happier, the more grateful and the more loving you are, the better you attract. The more active you are, the more your activities reflect the realization of your dreams, the more you forward the process. And remember: only focus on what you want. Never, never, never, never think of or focus on unwanted things. Because with your focusing on them, you attract them.

For that reason it is a good idea to avoid all kinds of worry, every thought of lack, shortage, poverty, illness, enmity, failure, discord, childlessness etc. Once and for all you can wave good bye to those thoughts and establish a series of replacement images for the unwanted thoughts. Once you have replaced worry with gratitude, lack and shortage with abundance, poverty with wealth, illness with health, enmity with friendship, failure with success and discord with peace, you never have to worry about anything anymore. And the less you worry, the better you get at attracting what you want.

Or as Abraham says ironically: *"Feeling bad is the only thing you need to worry about!"* So, be happy, because then you attract happiness, health and abundance.

And don't be too hard on yourself. If you have done something that, seen in the rear view, wasn't all right, then learn from the mistake, realize that it was wrong and then forgive yourself. It doesn't help raise your vibration, and consequently that of the planet, that you are stuck in self reproach. Self reproach can easily lead to martyrdom, which leads to negative magnetizing of the blood and thus to a lack of health and happiness. Forgive yourself as you would forgive others.

Abraham is also a great advocate of not taking things so seriously. Don't make a drama out of trifles, which don't mean a thing tomorrow. Or with Abraham's words: *"Don't make such a big, hairy deal out of something that doesn't mean diddly squat"*. Relax and concentrate on finding things to cherish and try to see life from the humorous side. There is every reason to do that; we are eternal beings and we are part of the living universe; we are extensions of source energy or quanta of God, and it means that we are worthy, appreciated and of great importance to the whole. We don't have to prove anything. We are worthy by just existing. So we can just lean back and be happy to be alive. Right now we are living in fantastic and exciting times, where the technological progress has never been bigger, in more wealth and comfort than ever before, on a living planet where there is abundance and endless beauty, in a living universe where the basic tone is love.

"The Misery of the World"

"But how can we be happy, when there is so much misery in the world?" is what many people usually ask.

To that it can be said, as already mentioned previously, that the population of the Earth is standing on many, many different stages of development. But we are all without exception on our way to becoming finished, all-loving human beings. Nobody can avoid reaching that goal one day, and we are all, right now, at the peak of our development. That means that today we are more developed than we were yesterday. Every day we are shaped towards becoming more all-loving through our accumulation of experience, through our suffering and our karma. We become more all-loving in keeping with our shedding of our animal tendencies. And in keeping with our putting our animal tendencies behind us and becoming more and more all-loving, we create peace and harmony around us. We are quite simply living on a planet which is under development towards becoming a realm of peace. But the perfect, mature and ripe stage has not been reached yet. We can compare the population of the Earth with the apples on an apple tree. Some apples are close to being ripe, some apples are half ripe, and other apples are far from being ripe. Some apples are sweet, some are half sweet, some are half sour and some are still completely hard and sour.

But now it isn't so, that the sweet, ripe apples get worried about the presence of the unripe apples on the tree. Nor do they tell them that they should get ripe quickly, so that they themselves can be happy about being ripe. Nor do they say that the unripe apples cannot be on the tree, because their presence bothers them. The apples accept that not all are equally ripe. They know that there is very little that the ripe apples can do to help the unripe apples ripen quickly – only time can do that.

In the same way as there is nothing the ripe apples can do to help the unripe get ripe, in the same way there is very little that we, who live in peaceful and harmonious societies, can do to help those, who live in war and unrest, to get to where we are. We cannot force our peaceful and democratic societies on people who have not outlived their killing karma and who still strive for power to suppress others. It is the law of attraction that has seen to it that the war-loving people have got together in countries like Iraq and Sudan, and all our good intentions and efforts to help will drown, because a majority of those people is not ready to establish a peaceful and democratic society. It is the same as if the ripe apples would try to impose a premature ripe stage on the unripe apples - a stage to which they have not yet developed.

Now somebody might say: but it would be much better, if there was no war in this world, if there were no weapons, if there were no illnesses, if there was no terrorism, if there were no suicide bombers etc. But these things exist because they fit the stages of development that those, who make use of them, have reached. Abraham says that we live in a "well-stocked kitchen" – in a kitchen with a very big and varied stock of ingredients. No ingredient imaginable is missing from that kitchen.

But because of the large variety many people will say, *"But I don't like parsley, and it would be much better if parsley did not exist"*. And Abraham says, *"Parsley exists because many people want to use it, but that shouldn't bother you. Just don't put it in your pie"*. And you say, *"But it would be better, if parsley didn't exist."* And Abraham, *"Just don't put it in your pie"*. You, *"But I would be happier if parsley were exterminated"*. Abraham, *"Just don't put it in your pie"*. You, *"But because parsley exists I can risk that it gets in my pie!"* Abraham, *"It can only get in your pie if you put it in yourself by constantly focusing on it!"* You, *"Look now it got in my pie!"* Abraham, *"It got in your pie because you put it there by constantly focusing on it! You didn't have to put it there! You could just have ignored it."*

The fact that there are many ingredients in the kitchen, including some that we may not like, is only a problem to those who do not know how to focus. Because we have the ability to focus, we can just avoid focusing on the things we don't like. It is much better for us and for the vibration of the Earth in general, if we only focus on things we like. By focusing on things we don't like, we attract them and in that way they can influence our lives. Therefore: Don't focus on the unwanted!

It really shouldn't worry us that there are many ingredients in "the kitchen". We can just avoid using the ones we don't like. It is not the problem of a peace-loving human being that terrorism exists. Because in keeping with the peace-loving being's cleansing of his mentality of murderous energies, he cannot attract those energies. In the mentality of the peace-loving being there is nothing with which to attract the murderous energies. You cannot attract something with nothing. And consequently you are protected from being the victim of a terror attack. Then you are protected by your own karma and the strongest force in the universe: The law of attraction. This means that you cannot attract energies that do not match energies in your own vibration. When you don't have murderous energies in your own vibration, you cannot attract them. There is no better protection. And there is no other protection.

The thing is that there is very little we can do to save the world. And both Martinus and Abraham emphasize, proclaim and insist that the world does not need saving. Everything is, as already mentioned, completely as it should be. We have not come down here to save anybody or anything. We have come down here to work on our own perfection. Martinus says that world peace begins in the heart of each and every one of us.

"To those human beings who, of all their heart, want peace, it can often be difficult to see where, in times like these, they should intervene in order to produce the right effects, and many just give up. But you shouldn't give up, you shouldn't just let your hands be idle and think that there is nothing you can do. <u>The individual human being must work to create peace in his own consciousness, and only then does he get the ability to affect his surroundings and thus help create peace and harmony around him.</u> But it is a prerequisite, an absolute necessity, first to have peace in your own heart, so that you don't feel antipathy against anybody or anything." (Martinus: "Freedom – Emancipation and Peace", Kosmos 3, 1993, my underlining added).

The only thing you have to do is to cleanse your own thought sphere and try to exterminate your own animal tendencies. Part of this extermination is not to feel antipathy towards anybody or anything. When you are able to radiate tolerance, understanding, gratitude and love, then this positive radiance will affect the surroundings positively and create harmony around you. And thus you have helped raise the vibration on Earth a little bit. But every little bit counts.

So, we have to start by creating peace in our own hearts and in our own consciousness. That is all we have to do. And when enough of us have created peace in our hearts, world peace will eventually come, because then the law of attraction will see to it that the peace-loving beings will get together with other peace-loving beings, and in that way they will attract more peace-loving beings and thus the realm of the peace-loving beings will grow and grow.

The law of attraction sees to it that nobody lives under circumstances that they have not attracted themselves. Consequently everybody is right where he or she should be in order to work best for his own development towards perfection. Everything is truly very good.

Part II

The Law of Attraction in the Process of Reincarnation and after "Death".

1. Introduction to Part II

We have now seen how the law of attraction works in our daily lives and in our destiny, but as the law of attraction is the strongest natural force in the universe, it is obvious that the law is also effective in a number of other areas. Actually we can say that there are no areas in which the law is not effective.

In order to make the picture of the workings of the law of attraction more complete, we shall, in the following chapters, look at some select areas where the law has a great importance. We shall look at how the gravity of the Earth is a result of the law of attraction in action, and we shall look at the role played by this law in connection with the process of reincarnation and in connection with our destiny after the death of our physical body.

Furthermore, we shall see how we, with our wishes and longings, shape the societies of the future, just as it is the wishes and desires of past generations that have shaped the societies we have today.

Here in part two we mostly rely on the Martinus material, as Abraham does not have as many specifics about these subjects as Martinus. However, Abraham certainly agrees on the basic ideas: that the Earth is a living being, that thoughts come before any material manifestations, that reincarnation is a fact, that there is no death, that we are all part of a living, conscious universe and that there is a divine plan behind our existence. Although the two sources focus on different aspects they agree on all the fundamental points.

2. The Earth

The Earth Is a Living Being

Today it is generally assumed that we live on a dead planet, but even if this is practically viewed as a scientific fact, there is not a shadow of proof for the validity of this claim. On the contrary, everywhere there is visible, tangible proof that the Earth is alive. We shall look at the proof in this chapter.

The Moon is a Planet Corpse

If the Earth really was dead, it would look like the Moon. Actually the Moon is, according to Martinus, a planet corpse, which means the physical body of a planet whose "I" or spiritual force has left. The Moon is dead as a door nail. There is no life on it: not a bacterium, not an insect, not a plant, not an animal, no atmosphere and no magnetic field. If the Earth was really as dead as it is claimed, it would look like the Moon. Then we couldn't live here. Then no life forms could live here.

The Earth's Manifestation as Alive

The Earth is a living being. Martinus explains in the book "On Funerals", chapters 83 to 87 in which ways the Earth manifests itself as a living being.

It has a skeleton in the shape of the firm mineral parts (mountains and mountain ranges), on which the softer parts, the layers of soil, rest. The layers of soil are comparable to our musculature, and in these there is an immense process of transformation of matter or metabolism taking place. This transformation of matter is comparable to the one that takes place in our own organism. Metabolism means combustion and transformation of matter or energy, and without metabolism, no vital functions. The fact that there is a transformation of matter is a sign of life.

On the surface of the Earth there is constantly an enormous transformation of matter in the shape of the cyclic breaking down of matter: organic matter is broken down and is reduced to mould in order to be, at a later time, absorbed as nourishment in plants and be part of a new cycle. This transformation of matter or metabolism is a life function just as our own metabolism and it is a tangible proof that the Earth is living being. A dead being has no metabolism.

The water on the surface of the Earth is comparable to the blood of the planet, which through large and small "arteries", waterways, streams, brooks, and rivers transports this liquid around on the whole surface of the globe. Also the water has a cycle via evaporation through heating and condensation and precipitation through cooling. This cycle is comparable to the huge breathing of the Earth giant.

The Earth also eats, it eats all day. Its food consists of the particles that, in immense amounts, are constantly emitted from the Sun in the shape of light particles. The sea of light is the material food of the planet.

The many natural forces: winds, storms, hurricanes, breezes, rain, cold and heat are aspects of the life functions of the giant, its digestion and metabolism.

And just as our organism consists of a an endless amount of micro organisms in the shape of organs, cells, molecules, atoms, etc,, which all are living beings, also the Earth has an enormously rich micro life in the shape of humans, animals, fish, birds, insects, plants, mosses, algae, bacteria etc. The Earth is as alive as we are, and its body is the home of en endless amount of living beings, in complete analogy with our own bodies, which are the home of billions and billions of living micro organisms.

The fact that the bodily shape of the Earth is very different to ours does not deprive it of the possibility of being alive, because the manifestations of life are more than plentiful. We see a small proof of this by observing the countless, totally different life forms that inhabit the Earth in both micro- and meso cosmos. One only has to mention the following life forms to establish that life has no specific preferences with regard to shape: a jelly fish, a giraffe, an ant, a lizard, a sea anemone, a cactus, a slipper animalcule, a hammer head shark, a beetle, an ash tree, a fern and an algae. None of these living beings have identical shapes and yet no one would hesitate to accept them as alive.

The Micro Beings of the Earth

Just as our body is full to the brim with micro beings (organs, nerves, cells, molecules etc.) so is the Earth full of micro beings in the shape of plants, animal and humans. We could not be alive without our micro cosmos and neither could the Earth without its microcosmos. Through the law of attraction the Earth has attracted exactly the mix of individuals that fits its mentality at its present level of evolution. When the Earth has the mix of living beings that it has at the moment then it is because it has attracted them with its consciousness forces. This mix is an exact match to the present mentality of the Earth. The human beings are the brain cells of the planet and it needs us, indeed we are absolutely essential to the planet.

For that reason the Earth protects us, its micro individuals.

The Bodily Functions of the Earth and Its Protection of Its Micro Individuals

But not only that. If the Earth was not a living being, which regulates the functions of its body just as we regulate all the functions of our body, who, then, is it that sees to it that the oxygen level is always around 21 % in spite of the fact that the number of living beings on the planet is rising and in spite of the fact that the burning of fossil fuels consumes oxygen? Somebody is seeing to it that the oxygen level of the air is always constant no matter how much oxygen is consumed. There is also somebody that sees to it that the salinity of the seas is constant. The constancy in these two factors would not be possible, if they were not regulated. And who other than a living being could regulate something? This regulation is done by the Earth being and for that reason they are kept constant.

That a regulation is taking place of the oxygen- and carbon dioxide contents of the atmosphere has not gone unnoticed. In the February 2004 issue of the monthly magazine "National Geographic" one could read a 30 page long article titled *"The Case of the Missing Carbon"*. The article illustrates that there are forces at work on the planet that are regulating the natural processes. The author of the article does not understand what it is that is regulating these processes, but can only observe that something inexplicable is taking place.

According to the article there is too little carbon dioxide. Way too little. There ought to be the double amount of CO_2 in the atmosphere, when the various forms of pollution, combustion and contamination are taken into consideration. Where has all that CO_2 gone? It really is a mystery. The article with its many data is tangible proof that there are forces at work that are much greater than any scientist had imagined in his wildest dreams. This is what it says:

"Start the car, turn on a light, adjust the thermostat, or do just about anything, and you add carbon dioxide to the atmosphere. If you're an average resident of the United States, your contribution adds up to more than five metric tons of carbon a year.

The coal, oil, and natural gas that drive the industrial world's economy all contain carbon inhaled by plants hundreds of millions of years ago – carbon that now is returning to the atmosphere through smokestacks and exhaust pipes, joining emissions from forests burned to clear land in poorer countries. Carbon dioxide is foremost in an array of gases from human activity that increase the atmosphere's ability to trap heat. (Methane from cattle, rice fields, and landfills, and the chlorofluorocarbons in some refrigerators and air conditioners are others.) Few scientists doubt that this greenhouse warming of the atmosphere is already taking hold. Melting glaciers, earlier springs, and a steady rise in global average temperature are just some of its harbingers.

By rights it should be worse. Each year humanity dumps roughly 8 billion metric tons of carbon into the atmosphere, 6.5 billion tons from fossil fuels and 1.5 billion from deforestation. But less than half the total, 3.2 billion tons, remains in the atmosphere to warm the planet. Where is the missing carbon? "It's a really major mystery, if you think about it," says Wofsy, an atmospheric scientist at Harvard University. His research site in the Harvard Forest is apparently not the only place where nature is breathing deep and helping save us from ourselves. Forests, grasslands, and the water of the oceans must be acting as carbon sinks. They steal back roughly half of the carbon dioxide we emit, slowing its buildup in the atmosphere and delaying the effects on the climate." (National Geographic, February 2004, page 94).

What we are witnessing is that every year 4.8 billion cubic tons of carbon dioxide go "missing" and has mysteriously been disposed of. It is, as the atmospheric scientist Mr. Wofsy says, *"a really major mystery"*. Where does all that carbon dioxide go?

The article lists four possible answers to this question. The perma frost of the poles is the "storage" of about 14 % of the carbon dioxide on Earth. The waters of the North Atlantic absorb 500 million cubic tons, the forests of the Northern hemisphere constitute the planet's biggest "absorber" of carbon dioxide and the tropical forests take care of about 35 % of the carbon that is constantly circulating between the Earth and the air. Still these "sinks" cannot explain where all the missing carbon dioxide has gone.

And then there is the problem that when all the carbon dioxide is absorbed by plants, which then transform it into oxygen, well, then the content of oxygen of the air should rise correspondingly. But it doesn't. The oxygen content of the air is precisely where it has always been. That is another mystery. The author of the article admits that we are witnessing that Nature is giving us a helping hand.

But with such a realization, written in big, red font across page 103, ("Nature's helping hand") it should not be too far away that somebody realizes that there has to be a living entity behind this regulating, this "great gift", that Nature is giving Mankind. Because what other than some living entity can give somebody a helping hand? What other than a living entity can regulate and "tamper with" the carbon dioxide level? However, the author of the article does not seem to be able to conclude that it has to be a living being with consciousness and will that is regulating the levels of carbon dioxide and oxygen of the atmosphere.

Let us have a look at what Martinus says about the "helping hand" of the Earth being to us, its micro beings.

"As no living being can exist without being a macro being to its micro beings, and this, again, repeats itself when it comes to the micro beings, as these are also macro beings to the micro beings in their organism, it becomes a fact that <u>all living beings, as already mentioned, are subject to a cosmic principle of protection.</u> As it is thus of vital importance to the macro being to protect the micro beings in its own organism, the concept that we call "Providence" becomes a living, inevitable fact. In this way all living beings are subject to a principle of protection from a Providence. The humans, animals, plants and minerals of the planet are organic parts of the huge body that we call The Earth. Thus the Earth is a living being and constitutes our macro being and is subject to a vital condition of such a being: to protect the micro beings in its organism".
(Martinus: LB VI (The Book of Life, volume 6), paragraph 2025, my underlining added).

Here we see that micro beings are subject to a cosmic principle of protection and even that it is a vital condition to the macro being to exert this protection. Because, by exerting this protection, the macro being also defends its own existence and experience of life, so it is quite logical that it has to be like that. The macro being simply cannot help protecting its micro beings. This happens in exactly the same way in our own organism, where our "I" also helps the micro organisms fight an infection by raising the temperature of the body. When we have a fever, we help our micro organisms kill an intruding enemy. And thus we help both ourselves and the micro beings.

There is a constant communication between the micro beings and their macro being and a few examples could be: when we yawn, it is a sign that our micro beings are telling us that they need a rest. When we have a pain in the stomach, it is usually a sign that our micro beings are telling us that we have eaten something that they are not happy with and whose digestion causes them pain. When we are feeling hungry, it is a sign that our micro beings are telling us that they need fuel, so could we please eat something. When we feel ill with e.g. the flu, it is a sign that our micro beings are telling us that they need us to rest, so that they can better deal with the fighting off of the intruding enemy. It is normally so that the macro being heeds the pleas of the micro beings and acts accordingly. In that way the macro being protects its micro beings and functions as a kind of providence to them. This principle is exactly the same in our relationship to our macro being, the Earth, and even if we are not yet very good at noticing and interpreting this communication, there is no doubt that the Earth is responding to our pleas. Hence the missing carbon.

On the basis of the above Martinus quotation we can state that it is the Earth giant itself that we can thank for the disappearance of the carbon dioxide. Nothing less. The 4,8 billion cubic tons of missing carbon dioxide not only indicate that the Earth is a living being that regulates the conditions in its body, but also that all the living beings that are inhabiting the globe right now are subject to a cosmic principle of protection. Greater forces are at play than any of us ever dreamt about. We are definitely not alone and unprotected, but are living under the protective wings of our macro being.

On the experience of life of the "I" and the forces of nature as expressions of the bodily functions of a living being Martinus says:

"The surrounding Nature is thus not dead, random forces to us, just as our internal organic functions: digestion, blood circulation, glandular- and thought functions are not random. They are living, organic manifestations, through which a macro being is able to sustain its experience of life in the same way as our organism is a tool through which we are able to experience life. Our experience of life is thus a very intimate relationship between the three indelible facts: micro cosmos, meso cosmos and macro cosmos". (Martinus: LB VI, section 2026).

The regulation of the amounts of oxygen and carbon dioxide in the atmosphere are living, organic manifestations that are necessary for the Earth being in order to maintain its health and consequently its experience of life. The "I" of the Earth can and will regulate these things both for its own and for our sakes.

"Here we have pointed out a few factors that show that the Earth, the extensive globe that we are living on, is not a dead lump of matter, and that the prominent realities that we call "natural forces" are not random, useless phenomena, but are the vital functions of a living being, completely analogous to the life functions and movements of our own organism, and that the Earth is thus a living being. Indeed, this is so evident that it does not depend on any type of cosmic perspicacity, but will become the logic, based on intelligence, that any scientific investigation will eventually confirm". (Martinus: "On Funerals, chapter 86).

That the Earth is a living being is so evident that it does not require any type of cosmic perspicacity. It can simply be observed through the fact that there is life everywhere on the planet, and through the fact that there is movement both from the interior of the planet through volcanic eruptions and earth quakes, and on its surface in the shape of breeze, wind, storms, hurricanes, typhoons, electrical discharges etc. Furthermore there is a constant metabolism in the shape of the circulation of matter, and a well- known and well- described circulation of water. If we want to know what a dead planet looks like, we can just look at the Moon. It is dead. The Earth is alive.

The Aura of the Earth

Because the Earth is a living being it has, just as we have, an electromagnetic field, or aura, which surrounds its physical body. This electromagnetic field is known as the magnetic field of the Earth, and even though the science of physics has known of its existence for many years, it has not been able to explain what the magnetic field is and where it comes from. Albert Einstein considered the origin of the magnetic field of the Earth as one of the three most important unsolved riddles of physics.

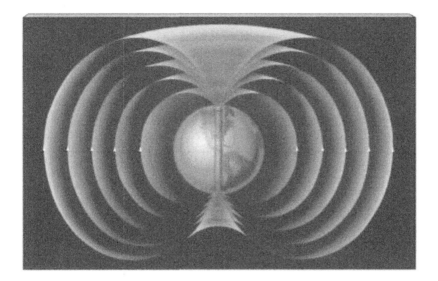

The Earth's magnetic field as it would look if it were symmetrical (source ESA).

The magnetic field of the Earth is in reality identical to its aura or spiritual forces. Because the Earth is a living being it has spirit, consciousness and will in exactly the same way as we have. The Earth thinks, decides, wishes, and ponders, just as we do. There is in principle no difference between our spirit, consciousness and will and the spirit, consciousness and will of the Earth. The only difference is that the spiritual forces of the Earth are much stronger than ours, as their strength naturally has to be adapted to the giant being that the Earth is in comparison to us. Our spiritual forces are of an electrical nature, and so, of course, are those of the Earth. They are only far stronger than ours, indeed so strong that an electrical discharge from the spiritual forces of the Earth in the shape of lightening can kill a man or an animal.

Gravity

It is the spiritual forces of the Earth that are responsible for gravity. Because the Earth has both consciousness and will, it attracts, through the law of attraction, everything that is on wavelength with its own spiritual forces. This again means that the Earth, with the force of its will born by wishes and desires, has attracted the living beings that are living here today. It is no chance occurrence that the beings, us humans included, that live on the Earth today, are here right now. We have reincarnated here because our own spiritual forces have been attracted to the spiritual forces of precisely this planet, because the two sets of spirit are on wavelength. The law of attraction is active at all times and in all dimensions and magnitudes, and it is this law that has the final say as to which planet we reincarnate on. We have reincarnated here, because our consciousness and spirit are on wavelength with the consciousness and spirit of the Earth being.

Let us have a look at what Martinus has to say about the relation between our will and that of the Earth:

"We see a very tangible proof of this "will power" in the shape of what we call "gravity". The mentioned force is again the same as the force that determines that a thing "falls" towards the Earth. This force is nothing less than the "will" of the Earth "I" and the attraction it exerts via its "I" towards the energies of which its physical organism (the Earth globe) consist. This "organism" is again the same as a combination of matter, solely maintained through the desire or attraction of the Earth "I". It is this force that determines that a thing has "weight". We can witness that we have exactly the same force in our interior, when we, for instance, "lift" something. The force with which we "lift" is nothing less than our own "gravity", released by our "I" in our own organism". But here we do not call it "gravity", but express it as our "will".

"All "fall force" in nature is thus maintained by the "will" of the "Earth I," while our own "lifting" of something is maintained by our own "will". Just as the "fall force" in nature is "gravity" to us, our own "lifting" of something is gravity to the thing that is being lifted. In this way we see two kinds of gravity. We can call the former "macro cosmic gravity" and the latter "meso cosmic gravity", depending on which "cosmos" they derive from respectively". (Martinus: LB II, paragraphs 524 and 525 (extracts)).

Here Martinus points out that there is both macro cosmic gravity, or the one we learned about in our physics lessons as Gravity, and meso cosmic gravity, which is the force that emanates from us. Both these types of gravity are results of the will of living beings. It is easy to see in our own case, because when we through our will want to lift a thing, this will of ours becomes gravity to the thing that is being lifted. Gravity and attraction are results of the wills of living beings. The gravity and magnetic field of the Earth show that the Earth is alive.

The Climate of the Earth

Naturally, it is also the "I" of the Earth that regulates the climate here, and it is a well known fact that the climate has never been constant. There have been periods, when it was much colder than now (ice ages), and periods where the climate was far warmer than now. Actually, the climate of the Earth has, over the last 2 billion years, oscillated between cold (we are now in a cold climate period) and very hot, as it was, for instance, 65 million years ago, when the dinosaurs lived. In the late trias period (about 250 million years ago) there was no ice on neither the North nor the South Pole, and it can be mentioned, that where the North Sea is today, there was once a tropical savanna (11). Nothing on the face of the Earth is constant, because everything is subject to the bodily functions of a living being and its thought climate. Life means movement and movement means change.

With regards to global warming let it be said again: one cannot with any right worry about global warming as long as one is ignorant about the greatest factor of all that regulates the climate, viz: the fact that the Earth is a living being. The climate is under the control of the Earth being and as long as one doesn't realize that, and as long as one believes that we live on a dead planet, one cannot with any weight speak about the reasons for the state of the climate and the planet. When one claims that the slightly warmer climate that we are experiencing right now (12) is solely due to human factors, one has indeed reckoned without one's host.

Because the Earth is a living being with will, wishes and desires, just as we are, and because the Earth being regulates its bodily functions just as we do, it is, as already mentioned, completely unnecessary and futile for us, the micro beings of the Earth, to worry about the climate. It is constantly being regulated by the Earth itself in conjunction with the Sun. Any kind of worry about the climate is inappropriate, because by worrying one attracts what one worries about.

That does not mean, however, that we should not treat the planet and the resources with respect and economize with them. It seems like a good idea to spend the resources wisely, recycle, save, conserve energy, invest in sustainable energy, pollute less and develop new sources of energy.

Energy Sources

Martinus writes again and again, over and over that everything is very good. He can say so, because development is advancing according to plan and because we are well on the way to becoming real, altruistic human beings. But because we still haven't reached that high goal, there are still unfinished manifestations everywhere, carried out by beings, who still haven't outlived their animal tendencies and consequently are still able to vandalize, go to war, carry out terrorism, have a lust for power, want revenge, are greedy and ruthless. But because we reap as we sow, unrest and war will exterminate itself, and it is "only" an expression of a certain stage of development.

In the posthumously published book (2004) "The intellectualized Christianity", which was among the last things Martinus wrote before he passed away in 1981, he does, however, present a very serious warning to Mankind – probably the most serious in all of his production: against nuclear power.

Today there is a tendency to look upon nuclear power as a lesser evil than the burning of fossil fuels, as nuclear power does not entail emissions of carbon dioxide. But that is a very wrong assessment. Nuclear waste is a product that is completely indigestible to the Earth; it stops the metabolism and circulation of matter in the areas affected. It is so indigestible that the metabolism of the Earth is blocked, indeed sabotaged, in the areas where it is stored. As the waste furthermore has a longer "shell life" than the material that it is encapsulated in, it will create huge problems when the packaging decomposes.

"The Earth is a healthy, living organism for a macro being, in which all the living beings of the Earth are micro beings and meso beings. If they are prevented from carrying out their normal function, the macro being will feel ill to a similar extent. Haven't many human organisms died because their micro beings didn't function as they should? –Why would this be any different with the Earth, which is a living being in a higher spiral? – Mankind has enabled himself to sabotage the cycle of the Earth's life force. Thus it has introduced a force that is millions of times greater than their own little micro cosmic force, but they don't know what they are doing or in which danger they are living. Man thinks that he can use this force as an everyday energy source for his industry and other needs for power or energy, instead of the power sources provided by nature: water, air, coal, oil and electricity. These materials do not stop the circulation of matter as the life force waste of the Earth does. The latter type of waste is taken out of circulation and it will consequently accumulate. How does this help the health of the Earth, even if one can, for a limited period of time, give this waste an isolated burial? What about the possibilities of life for the living beings that are living in the affected areas, when the lethal waste has survived the perishable nature or dissolution of the packaging material, whether

it is at sea or on land?" (Martinus: "The Intellectualized Christianity", chapter 1, paragraph 9).

Even though we pack and wrap the nuclear waste really, really well it will inevitably be so that the packaging material will perish before the nuclear waste, and it will create insurmountable problems for the living beings that will live in the affected areas when the time comes. Now, somebody might be of the opinion that it is not our problem, because it is way out in the future, but we cannot look upon it like that. Partly because we ourselves will reap the seeds we have thus sowed, because we are eternal beings who will experience the consequences of our deeds. And partly we risk causing illnesses in the organism of the Earth with the consequences that this may have for life on the planet.

According to Martinus the power sources provided by nature for man are water, air, coal, oil and electricity. These energy sources do not sabotage the metabolism of the Earth, and we saw that it seems that the Earth itself can counteract our excessive emissions of carbon dioxide.

And we are not in shortage of energy. Every day the Earth receives 14.000 times more energy than we need form the Sun. It seems like a really good idea to work at getting better at exploiting this abundance to cover our present energy needs.

In the future there will be no energy problems whatsoever. Martinus is said to have declared (13) that in the future we will make a series of discoveries that will enable us to tap energy in unlimited amounts from the so-called vacuum or "empty space" with a simple gadget resembling an ordinary antenna. Already now it has been acknowledged within the field of quantum physics that "empty space" is anything but empty, but contains huge amounts of energy, indeed that "empty space" is an inexhaustible energy ocean. The question is "just" how to exploit it.

3. Our Entire Human Civilization Is Materialized Thoughts

Thought Comes First

The fact that thoughts are "something" which is of extreme importance becomes clear when we realize that our entire civilization is in reality materialized thoughts. A thing can only be created on the basis of a thought or a mental picture. The thought construction always comes before any kind of physical creation. We can only make a chair on the basis of a thought about how the chair should look, we can only build a house on the basis of a thought about what the house should look like, we can only construct a computer on the basis of a thought about how it should be made etc. All manmade things were a thought before they became a physical creation. In most cases we will make a drawing of the idea in our head before we start on the actual construction, but that does not change the principle that it is thought first. When all manmade things were a thought before they became tangible, physical objects (and there are no exceptions here), it becomes clear that our entire civilization is materialized thoughts – thoughts that have been "carried out" and become physical manifestations.

"The entire modern civilization is manifested thoughts, which in reality means materialized thoughts. Materialization is not something that only takes place at certain spiritualist séances, you see; all physical creation is in reality variations of materialization....An example of such a slow materialization is the creation of one of Mankind's technical masterpieces, a bridge across an abyss or something similar. Thought is added to thought in the consciousness of the technician, the strength of the construction is carefully calculated, a large amount of drawings are created, perhaps also a model, and many other stages are passed in the process before the finished bridge can carry human beings across the abyss. But this finished bridge is materialized thoughts, even if it took several years to materialize them. An example of fast materialization in our daily lives is the radio. The thoughts of the speaker are materialized into words, i.e. to specific sound waves, which again are dematerialized by the microphone and with incredible speed pass through the air. Our radio receiver rematerializes the radio waves to sound waves, which hit our ears and via our nervous system and our consciousness the sound waves are dematerialized again and become thoughts. Something as ordinary as the building of bridges and broadcasting is in reality associated with something that human beings would normally call supernatural. In the same way much of what humans call supernatural is quite

natural when they gradually become acquainted with the laws that define these so-called supernatural phenomena." (Martinus: "Death and Man's Mental World", Kosmos 4, 1992).

Materialization and Dematerialization

Before we return to the theme of our civilization we should have a quick look at what Martinus says in the above quotation about materialization and dematerialization in connection with radio transmissions. When something is dematerialized it enters the ray-formed state, i.e. the state of matter in which most of the electromagnetic spectrum exists: invisible waves and rays. The sound waves that come from the vocal cords of the speaker are picked up by the microphone and are transformed into electromagnetic radiation. Thus they are dematerialized in the sense that they can no longer be perceived by the physical senses. The sound waves have been transformed into electromagnetic radiation.

All electromagnetic radiation moves at the speed of light, and it means that the radio waves can move as fast as light across huge distances. When you tune your radio receiver to the wavelength that corresponds to the program you want to hear, then the radio receiver sees to it that the radio wave can rematerialize, i.e. become perceptible to the physical senses again. In the radio the electromagnetic waves have been transformed into sound waves, so now we can hear what the speaker says, and the whole transmission of the sound takes place via dematerialization and rematerialization with such an enormous speed that we perceive it as if it all took place at once. Then, when the sound waves hit our ear, they are dematerialized in our brain and become thoughts. Only then have we understood the content of what has been transmitted. It also means that we are making constant use of materialization and de-materialization.

Also all conversations take place using materialization and dematerialization. When we have something to tell our interlocutor, it will always be on the basis of a thought. As already mentioned, a thought consists of electromagnetic radiation and is in this sense non-material. When we have something to say, we materialize our thoughts via our vocal cords and articulation instruments, and in that way the thought gets a physical expression – the thought has now been materialized and has become a sound wave, which can be perceived by the ear of our interlocutor. Via the ear the sound wave is dematerialized and becomes a thought in the brain of our interlocutor. A totally normal conversation is consequently a situation where thoughts are materialized and dematerialized at great speed, and we are so used to this mechanism that we don't realize what a complicated process and sophisticated apparatus we are making use of. But it is a fact that materialization and dematerialization is something very commonplace.

The Thoughts of Former Generations

When our whole civilization is materialized thoughts it does, of course, mean that the society we are living in today is the materialized thoughts of the generations that came before us.

"Why is it that human beings of today have been able to make the natural forces work for them? Why do we live in lovely houses, that shelter us from wind and rain, and which can be heated in winter and where we can turn the light on when it gets dark? Why can we fly through the air and sail both above and below the surface of the sea and in many other ways move quickly through space? Because we have wanted it, we have longed to have such a mastery of the natural forces. But how have we been able to nourish these longings and wishes? Well, obviously when we did not have the technical and scientific know how that we have now. When we were primitive Stone Age people who lived in dark caves and had to put up a desperate fight to stay alive, that is when the first longings for a more independent way of life arose, where we would not so easily succumb to the supremacy of nature.

Obviously the Stone Age man did not have the ability to wish electrical light, central heating, cars, air planes etc. All these details in the civilization picture have only arisen in later times in the thoughts and dreams of men, as they gradually began to make technical and scientific progress. But the longing for a life where all the "demonic" forces that man had to fight against had been conquered, has been the driving force that gave birth to today's technical and scientific triumphs. It does not mean that these wishes and longings have only been inherited from generation to generation, that would be quite unjust, and from a cosmic point of view there is no injustice in the universe. Imagine, if the people of the stone age and other people of the past, who longed for a more comfortable life, were to die without ever having experienced a fraction of these comfortable life conditions, and then the people of today, who, if they had never lived before, would not have been able to have any wish or desire for comfort or pleasant life conditions, were born to the technical abilities and facilities of our technical times. This means that somebody, who were deeply longing for a more pleasant life, were to die without ever having experienced it, and some others, who had never had such wishes and desires, should have them quite undeservedly. That would be exceedingly unjust. But it certainly isn't like that. The people of the Stone Age, who longed to conquer the forces of nature and consequently have a better life, are the same as the modern people of today, who gradually, with respect to the purely physical and practical, have achieved such a life." (Martinus: "Longing", Kosmos 2, 2003).

When today we enjoy an endless number of technical benefits, which make our life much easier and much more pleasant than that of former generations, well, then it is because it is the materialized thoughts of former generations that we have the pleasure of enjoying. But as we are eternal beings that have "worked our way up" through the times from primitive Stone Age people to the more civilized human beings that we are today, well, then it is our own wishes and desires that we have now achieved. If things didn't work like that, then life would be exceedingly unjust, says Martinus, but it isn't. It is the fulfillment of our own wishes that we are now living. It is the results of our own desires that we are now reaping.

We can imagine that we, in a former incarnation, were sitting on a hard bench, freezing, in a small, cold cottage, where the wind came through every crevice. The work of the day had been done, and now there wasn't much to do. The fire was dying down, it was dark and the cold was creeping in. Now Sophie, who is sitting there freezing and bored in the dark, is thinking: How nice it would be, if we had proper light after the sun has set. How nice it would be if there was something that could entertain us. And how wonderful it would be if the heating just came without us having to go outside to chop more wood, which we first must fetch in the forest, where we first must fell a tree etc. With the emission of these wishes an energy is set in motion, which can only stop when the wishes have been fulfilled. And consequently we can, today, enjoy having radio, television, electrical light, central heating and all the other benefits, which modern civilization can offer.

It is with the wishes and longings that we nourish today that we create our own future and the civilization of that future.

We Create the Future with our Wishes

"It is not inconsequential what the individual human being is longing for nor what he or she does to gradually make the longings come true. The fact that modern human beings now have the possibility to get a theoretical overview of their life with respect to past and future incarnations, gives them the opportunity to see that they are the ones who have created the conditions that they are living under today through the desires, wishes and longings, which made them think and act as they did in the past. Thoughts and acts are force and energy, and all energy of the universe goes in cycles and creates cause and effect or fate. It is the longings, wishes and desires of the past that have created the present fate of the human beings. But the human beings are still able to create fate, because today they are creating their future both with respect to

what they are going to experience in life after death and in their coming physical incarnations. *What they are longing for, they will get to experience, as soon as their fate pattern makes room for these experiences. No human being must in the great cosmic cycle experience more happiness or more suffering than any other. Providence has no favorites, and nobody is a scapegoat. It is the living beings' own longings that drive them forwards in development, i.e. through the many different thought climates of experience towards new longings and new experiences "* (Martinus: "Longing", Kosmos 2, 2003, my underlining added).

So, it is today that we create our future through the thoughts we are thinking and the longings and desires we have. We shall come back to the question of life after death in chapter 5, so let us just have a look at the question of the favorites and scapegoats of Providence.

As we are eternal beings we are, as already mentioned, on a never-ending journey through physical and spiritual realms. We shall come back to the spiritual realms. We, who are incarnated here on Earth right now, are on our way to becoming Man in the image and likeness of God. We are coming from the animal kingdom, where our ability to survive depended on selfish behavior and egoism. Slowly, through many, many thousands of incarnations, we are working our way away from egoism in order to become real, all-loving human beings. With our practicing of egoism we have sown a lot of karma, which will return to us as fate.

When we are in the middle of the reaping of dark fate, which can come to us in the shape of illnesses, accidents, handicaps, imprisonment, war scenarios, miserable life conditions etc., it is easy to fall victim to the misperception that we are the scapegoats of fate and that life is extremely unjust. But our fate is an expression of the highest justice, and we cannot live under circumstances that we haven't created ourselves through our acts and attraction. Consequently there are no scapegoats and Providence has no favorites either. Everybody must go through the same to become the same. When he, who feels betrayed by fate, sees somebody, who is living in prosperity and happiness, then he may think that that person is very fortunate and has been a favorite of fate, but that is not so. The suffering that the "scapegoat" is now living through, has either already been experienced by the "fortunate" person in a former incarnation, or is waiting for him in a future incarnation. *"No human being must, in the big cosmic cycle, experience more happiness or more suffering than any other"*. Life is totally just, but, of course, you cannot see that, if you think we only live one life. You cannot understand the fate of anybody, if you think that we only live once. Trying to understand one's fate in a one life perspective is like trying to understand the contents of a book written in a language you do not know.

The Spiritual World Is the Primary World

It is with our thoughts and wishes that we create, not only our destiny, but also the civilization of the future. It means that our thoughts are of enormous importance. Thoughts are spirit, which means non-physical matter. In our spiritual body or consciousness we have a whole world consisting of all possible thoughts, our memories, our plans for the future, our knowledge etc. Each and every one of us goes around with our own little spiritual world in our consciousness. It is our own spiritual world that sets the course for our future and our creations, and consequently it is clear that spirit has precedence over physical matter. It is always spirit or thought first. Without spirit or thought no physical thing could have come into being. That again means that it is the spiritual world that is the primary world and the physical world that is the secondary. Spirit, consciousness and thoughts came before the physical world and consequently it has priority over it. It is from spirit that everything physical has been created. The thought always comes before the physical materialization. There are no exceptions.

Also nature and everything that isn't manmade has been created on the basis of thoughts or spirit. When it is so in our world that even a pin has to have been a thought before it becomes a physical pin, then it is logical that the same principle must apply on a higher level. On the basis of the assumption that the method of creation that we know, viz. first idea and then physical creation, is also valid for what we can observe in nature, we can conclude that also the creations of nature have arisen on the basis of thoughts, spirit and consciousness. This conclusion is so much more obvious when you realize that a superior perfection can be observed in nature. In nature all matter goes in cycles, nothing goes to waste, everything is recycled and everything rests in a perfect balance. It can hardly be logical to conclude that the logical creations and the balance we see in nature should have come into existence from chaos on the basis of chance and random mutations. It is far more logical to conclude that also the creations of nature have arisen analogously to those of Man, i.e. through willful, conscious creation and intelligent planning.

The Intelligent Creator

All that we see in nature today is materialized thoughts conceived and created by a higher consciousness. As consciousness is invariably a characteristic of a living being, a higher being now appears. The physical matter we see in nature has been created on the basis of the thoughts and desires of a higher being. Everything without exception has been created on the basis of thought images founded in an intelligent plan. This not only becomes obvious when we consider the perfection and subtle balance of nature, but also when we observe the fantastic physical instrument that we are making use of: our own organism. The workings of this organism are so complicated, brilliant and impressive that we not even today have come to full clarity about how our organism works. To assume that something as complicated and perfect as that should have come into existence without intelligent planning is far, far out. It is illogical, disingenuous superstition disguised as science.

Through a simple analogy between creation in our own world and creation at a higher level an intelligent creator now appears. Without the superior mental capacity and willful planning of this creator the physical world could not have come into existence. Assuming that expedient and purposeful created things such as those of nature should have come into existence without a creator, only on the basis of chance and chaos is extremely naive. When it never happens in our world that a chair comes into existence on its own accord, how should this be possible in nature? Assuming that everything should have come into existence on its own without intelligent planning but solely based on chance occurrences is the same as assuming that a tornado can whirl through a scrap yard and at the same time assemble a jumbo jet. It is more naïve than the law permits.

There is no escaping the fact that spirit is something factual and that a spiritual world is in actual existence and there is no escaping the fact that a creator exists. What we call this creator is of no importance, and if we are tired of the word God, we can just call the creator something else. We can call "him" Jack, Brian or Evelyn, that is of no consequence, and "he" has no special preferences as to names, and "he" lacks the ability to become offended by our choice of name. But it is of importance that we acknowledge "his" existence. When it is of importance, it is because it would be helpful to our development that we get out of the spiritual darkness that we are living in right now. The godless, materialistic way of thinking based in the one life theory that is predominant in the west today is not particularly conveying for peace, global harmony and human happiness, just as it isn't conveying for any kind of understanding of why we are here or what the meaning of life is.

4. The Process of Reincarnation

We are eternal beings. Our existence has no beginning and can never end. Something that is eternal can neither have beginning nor ending. If it had, it wouldn't be eternal. Because we are tiny cells in the living, all-encompassing universe, our existence is as eternal as that of the universe.

Our primary and eternal form of existence is in spiritual matter. We always have a spiritual body, which by Martinus is denominated our eternal body. Our consciousness is eternally linked to this our spiritual body, indeed the two are identical. We have consciousness and ability to experience whether we are incarnated in a physical body or not. Our ability to experience never ceases.

"The mentioned eternal body forms a spiritual body in which the "I" of the individual manifests itself on a permanent basis, quite independently of whether it is discarnate or incarnated in a material or physical body... " (Martinus: "The Ideal Food", booklet 5, chapter 9).

In order that there can be basis for the experience of contrast on our eternal journey we must, at intervals, incarnate in the heavy, physical matter. That again means that we must link our "I" or consciousness to a physical body – we must reincarnate – become flesh again. The process of reincarnation has been meticulously described by Martinus, so in this chapter we shall see how it is possible that we can move from being spiritual beings to becoming physical beings. We shall also have a look at what decides which parents we are born to.

Where and with Whom Do We Reincarnate?

Do we choose our parents ourselves in a specific incarnation? Yes and no. It isn't so that we are sitting on a pink cloud looking at couples in love and then decide who we want as parents. But we do decide who it will be through who we have become. This again means that it is our specific vibration, whose wavelength reflects our thoughts on the basis of our accumulated mass of experience, which decides which parents we are attracted to. This attraction takes place automatically based on the law of attraction.

"When an individual is primarily born to parents with similar tendencies...this is naturally due to the law of attraction and repulsion. But in order to understand this we have to go all the way back to the discarnate state of that same individual, which means its spiritual existence before its birth in this life time. In the mentioned existence it appears, apart from in certain subordinate spiritual bodies, also in a general- or primary body. This body is described in "Livets Bog" as the "eternal body" of the individual or X2. ...As this very body thus appears as the seat of a continuously changing combination of

the basic energies, it consequently at all times represents a corresponding form of radiation. This radiation can again be expressed as the "spiritual halo" of the individual. This halo consists of spiritual energy. But as spiritual energy again according to "Livets Bog" comes under the concept of "electricity", the mentioned halo will thus represent some form of electrical nature. But an electrical amount of energy, which manifests in a certain limitation, can only be expressed as a "wavelength". But a "wavelength" can, again, only be directed by attraction and repulsion". (Martinus: "The Ideal Food", booklet 5, chapter 9).

We can imagine that we have our "I" and eternal body in the discarnate state, "sitting" in one of the spiritual realms. All incarnation in physical matter takes place from the kingdom of bliss, so let us say that our "I" is sitting in the said kingdom. Since the "I" left its last physical body behind through the process we call "death", a certain amount of time has passed, and now the "I" has a strong desire to return to the physical plane in order to get on in its development and renew its consciousness through the experience of contrast. The longing that the "I" is nourishing means that it radiates a fine, high-vibrating energy. It is this energy in combination with the proper energy of the "I" itself that is its point of attraction. So, the spiritual being that is ripe for reincarnation "is sitting" there radiating a certain electromagnetic wavelength and it can be said to be hoping that somebody will soon pick up its signal.

Physical beings normally do not have access to such a high-vibrating energy, so under normal circumstances they will not be able to get on wavelength with the discarnate "I". But during the sexual act and particularly during its culmination, the lovemaking couple radiate a very fine and high-vibrating energy, and it is this, during orgasm released energy that can "reach" the wavelength of the discarnate being and thus attract a suitable individual. By a suitable individual is meant a being that with respect to species, race and talent mass fits the joint energy release of the lovemaking couple.

"During the normal act of intercourse of two beings of opposite sex they radiate, as already mentioned, a spiritual aura or energy of bliss, which means that they, during the culmination of the act, unconsciously attain a wavelength similar to that of the energy of bliss of the discarnate beings that are ready for rebirth on the physical plane. The aura of every discarnate being is radiated from its set of talent kernels for physical creation, which begins to stir when its already mentioned maturity is attained. As the talent-kernel-sets of the beings are not equally advanced in development, their radiation of bliss or aura is also different. As the talent-kernel-sets of the physical intercourse-partners are also different, their radiation of bliss during the act of intercourse is also different. When a discarnate being is ripe for incarnation in physical matter, it is attracted to the normal act of intercourse of two physical beings, whose radiance of bliss is on the same wavelength as its own radiance of bliss. And through this contact

between the energy of bliss of the intercourse-partners and the energy of bliss of the discarnate being the process that we call conception takes place..." (Martinus: "The Eternal World Picture", volume IV, paragraph 34.18).

This means that the discarnate being is attracted to a love-making couple whose joint vibration is on wavelength with the vibration of the discarnate being. In order for the two sets of vibration to be on wavelength, they must be of the same species (cats are born to cats, pigs to pigs, humans to humans etc.), they must have a certain overlap of talent mass, more or less have the same moral standards and intelligence and more or less stand at the same level of development. Martinus points out that it is our own set of talent kernels and standard of development that determine which parents we are born to. Our set of talent kernels is the joint accumulation of talents, abilities, skills, experiences, dispositions, habits etc. that we have "reaped" in former incarnations. This material of experience is "stored" in our talent kernel set and it accompanies us from incarnation to incarnation. The accumulated "experience matter" is stored as electromagnetic radiation and it is this radiation, which determines to which love-making couple we are attracted during the sexual act. The law of attraction determines that we are born to beings that have a set of talent kernels which on a number of points matches our own. In order for the wavelengths to match and consequently attract each other, there has to be a certain amount of similarity in the talents between the discarnate being and its future parents. So, during conception there are not only two, but three sets of spiritual force present.

The Third Party of Conception

It is not possible to conceive a child only with an egg and a sperm cell. A third party is needed, and it is this third party which is the determinating factor in the development of the embryo and of the final form and details of the physical body that is now under creation.

"*The radiance from the sperm cells, introduced into the womb, and that of the egg cells already present there, is infected with the energy of bliss of the discarnate being. These cells or this fertilization material will hereafter consist of three sets of spiritual force, namely: one set from the male of the act of intercourse, one set from the female of the same act and the spiritual force of the discarnate being. When a thus infected sperm cell and egg cell combine, the discarnate spiritual being is attached to this combination in the womb. And here the aura or radiance from the sperm and egg cell is overshadowed by the aura or radiance of the discarnate being. The creation of a new physical organism begins. And the micro talents for the creation of a new physical organism, that are embedded in the sperm and egg cells from the intercourse-partners, will now gradually be more and more dominated by the spiritual force of the* *discarnate being*. *As this spiritual force is radiated from the talent kernel set of this being, it will gradually overtake the talent kernel sets from the intercourse-partners and the physical organism under creation will be continued completely* *in favor of the discarnate being. This creation of a new physical organism, which begins with the embryo in the womb and develops into a child ready to be born into the physical world, and which then continues its development into its fully grown state, is conveyed by three sets of talent kernels, each constituting one set of heredity. This again means: heredity from the talent kernel set of the male of the act of intercourse, heredity from the talent kernel set of the female of the act and heredity from the talent kernel set of the discarnate being. The two sets of talent kernels from the intercourse-partners are definitely not designed to complete the creation of the new physical organism. They are only initiators of* *this creation, which the discarnate being can overshadow and possess with the* *radiance of its set of talent kernels from former lives.*

(Martinus: The Eternal World Picture, IV, pages 20-23 (extracts), my underlining added).

In order for a discarnate being to be able to pass from the spiritual to the physical plane it needs a small amount of physical matter with which to initiate the creation of a physical body. It is this very small amount of physical matter that is "delivered" by the egg and sperm cells. But the egg and sperm cell cannot initiate the creation of the embryo on their own. Conception and creation of an embryo can only take place when a discarnate being with its spiritual force, its "I" and set of talents is attached to the egg that has been "infected" by the sperm cell in the womb. When this takes place there is, in effect, three sets of spiritual force present in the fertilized egg. But it is the spiritual force of the discarnate being which soon takes full control of the process of embryogenesis. The embryo will develop completely on the basis of the talents for bodily creation, which the discarnate being has developed and refined in former incarnations. This again means that the discarnate being now "just" continues where it let go the last time and creates a body completely in its own favor. The hereditary characteristics from the parents that are embedded in the sex cells only serve to initiate the process, and as soon as that has happened, the hereditary material from the parents will be of secondary importance in comparison to the "hereditary matter" which the discarnate being or the incoming soul brings with it in the shape of talents that it has cultivated and refined in former lives.

"From the moment that contact or connection is established between the egg- and sperm cell in the womb, the influence of the discarnate being becomes a total animation of the beginning embryogenesis. From this moment a small beginning embryo has thus incarnated, which in this way will be a beginning

physical body for its spirit." (Martinus: "The Eternal World Picture", volume IV, paragraph 34.20).

Embryogenesis can only take place when a third party participates in the process. It is this party that has the necessary "know how" of embryogenesis. The egg and the sperm cell have no idea how embryogenesis takes place, they only deliver the tiny, but necessary building block for the process to start. The "know how", which the incoming soul possesses, is something it has developed based in its experience with embryogenesis over many lives. It has quite simply done it before. It is this accumulated experience, which, as an automatic function, is embedded in the talent mass of the incoming soul. That means that the new body will be created completely at its discretion, or, as Martinus puts it *"completely in favor of the discarnate being."* So, it is the accumulated talent mass of the incoming soul that determines the final shape, form and content of the new organism, and not, as it is generally assumed, solely the genes of the parents. We can say that the parents place a certain hereditary mass, based in the genes, at the disposal of the incoming soul and that it "picks and chooses" in the genetic material and activates the genes that suit its own talent mass.

The Inheritance from One Self

So, it is the incoming soul that decides which genes are activated of the gene pool that the parents place at its disposal, and this picking from the gene pool is determined by the talents that the incoming soul has cultivated and refined during former incarnations. The new body under construction will be defined almost exclusively by the talent mass of the incoming soul. When children, just the same, have traits in common with the parents, this is due to the law of attraction and is not an actual inheritance from the parents.

"But here we have to understand that when children have the same abilities or talents as the parents, then these abilities or talents have not been inherited from the parents, but have already been developed by the beings in question in their former lives on Earth. It is thus absolutely their own inheritance and not something they get for free from the parents. And it is precisely the child's own inheritance from a former life, which causes it to become attached to parents with abilities and talents that are more or less related to its own, and thus it comes to resemble the parents with respect to species, race, talents and intelligence".(Martinus: The Eternal World Picture IV, paragraph 34.16)

The law of attraction sees to it that we are attracted to parents with a talent mass that is on wavelength with our own. So, when we have traits in common with our parents, it is because we have been attracted to the wavelength of those traits, and not because we have "just" been given these traits or inherited them "for free". When we are good at something this has solely been achieved through our own effort, and not just been "handed down". When we are born with talents for i.e. musical performance, with a gift for languages or a talent to paint, it is because we have practiced these talents in former incarnations. It is only through our own practicing of talents that we have become good at something. We don't get anything for free through inheritance.

So, we are attracted to parents whose joint radiation from their talent kernels is on wavelength with our own. But we also have to understand that there can practically never be a total match of talents. It is the joint, general wavelength of the parents that we are attracted to, but there will always be talents and skills that don't match. For that reason it is quite usual to see that children have talents that none of the parents have. A child can, for instance, have great artistic talents, which none of the parents possesses, it can have great mathematical skills, which none of the parents has, or it can have an intelligence that is far above that of the parents. These talents without a parental match cannot be explained by science, which only operates with genetic inheritance, but as in practically every child we see skills, dispositions and talents, which are not found in the parents, we can say that science has a problem explaining their origin. Where do these skills or talents come from? Have they just appeared by chance? Or through random mutations? No scientist can explain this. All our talents are a result of practice from former lives.

Hereditary Diseases

And how about diseases? There is a tendency to blame certain genes, when an individual is born with illnesses, and we usually call these diseases hereditary. But often the disease cannot be traced back to a parent, so where does the inheritance come from? Again, it comes from the individual itself, who in a former incarnation has acted in such a way that the talent kernels for the creation of a healthy organism have been damaged. Such a damaging takes place through an unnatural way of life and choice of unnatural stimulants.

"When I here give these simple, weak contours of the problem, it is only to show that no congenital tendencies have been caused undeservedly, but that these in absolutely all cases will be identical with results from the individual's own conduct in former lives or existences." (Martinus: "The Ideal Food", chapter 9).

When an individual is born with a bodily defect, this is due to the person having damaged his or her talents for the creation of a healthy organism in a former life. Such a damage of the talent kernels for health takes place through long and constant intake of "stimulants", that are foreign to the human organism. To such foreign stimulants belong all types of alcohol, tobacco and narcotics. Through dependency during a long life of these, to the human body totally unnatural substances, the talent kernels for the creation of a healthy body are broken down. And with demolished and defect talent kernels one can only create a defect organism.

When somebody is born with a defect organism, it is not due to a genetic defect, which the individual has been innocently imputed, but it is solely due to the individual's own "unwise play" with the energies. If it really was so that one could innocently be encumbered with serious disablement or insanity in a specific incarnation, then life would be exceedingly unjust. But it is not like that. Your state of health is a direct result of your conduct or dealing with the energies in a former incarnation.

"The good or bad tendencies of the individual have thus not been inherited from the parents, but are a direct "inheritance" from its former existence. This "inheritance" is stabilized or is released through the circumstances that the individual is attracted to parents within the same "wave area" or with the same tendencies". (Martinus: "The Ideal Food", chapter 10).

As we saw in chapter 6 the "I" is totally free with respect to all the energies. It can choose exactly the behavior it fancies. No divine hand reaches out from the wall to take the bottle away from the drunkard. All individuals "can afford" to make mistakes and mix the energies in an inappropriate way, because in eternity there is no lack of time. And when there is no lack of time, there is always the possibility to redo your choices and through the creation of experience learn to avoid mistakes. It is due to a lack of experience within a certain area that you "make a wrong pick" from the bag with the energies. The consequences of this wrong pick must, of course, be borne by the individual himself, because how would he or she get wiser otherwise? You wouldn't get wiser if your neighbor took the consequences of your actions.

The road back to health for the person, who through abuse has ruined his talents for the creation of a healthy organism, goes solely via a healthy way of life, and that means the intake of food that is natural to the human body, the intake of natural beverages and concentration on happy and healthy thoughts (14). It can take several incarnations to re-establish damaged talent kernels, but, as mentioned, one's natural health will gradually return in keeping with the upholding of a healthy and natural way of life.

Practice Makes Perfect

We all know that if we want to become good at something, then we have to practice. If we want to learn to play golf, well, then we must spend many hours on the practice course. And if we want to learn to speak Spanish, then we must practice, study, memorize and then practice some more. We know that if we want to learn something new, then it takes practice. We also know that we don't become good at anything by just lying on the sofa or hanging out on the street corner. We learn through practice and practice makes perfect.

We know and accept that that is how things work. When the only way to become good at something is via practice, well, then it is obvious that you, when you are born with a specific talent for something, necessarily must have been in a place before your birth, where you can have practiced the perfection of the specific talent. And what can such a place be other than a former life? In this way we can say that all our talents are irrefutable evidence that we have lived before. And in that way our former lives appear. We have had former lives in which we have practiced, cultivated and refined the talents that we are born with. Those talents are our inheritance from ourselves and have nothing to do with our parents.

But because of the law of attraction we are born to parents with a certain similarity in talent mass.

Artificial Insemination

Before we leave the all-important role played by the law of attraction in connection with the process of reincarnation, it would be relevant to take a look at how artificial insemination can take place.

We saw that it is the release of ecstatic energy from the intercourse partners during orgasm that attracts the discarnate being.

"When the act of intercourse can become the initiating factor for the incarnation of a spiritual being in physical matter... it is due to the divine, light aura that the normal act of intercourse between two one-poled beings of opposite sex releases. It is this aura that is felt by the partners as the culminating feeling of sensual pleasure they experience during intercourse. It constitutes the highest life force and is, as already described, no less than the holy spirit of God. This aura is of a spiritual nature and it has a specific wavelength for every single being and it normally only culminates during the act of intercourse...

When the normal act of intercourse between two beings of opposite sex takes place, the above-mentioned divine aura is released and the spiritual nature of this aura is identical to the aura, which the discarnate beings in the kingdom of bliss radiate. The kingdom of bliss is the plane where the discarnate beings are ripened for re-birth onto the physical plane."
(Martinus: "The Eternal World Picture" IV, pages 18-19).

The release of the orgasmic energy is of paramount importance to the attraction of the discarnate being and thus to fertilization, so the logical conclusion would be that artificial insemination cannot take place, as there is no orgasmic energy in the artificial process. But obviously artificial insemination does work, so how can it be explained that this process can produce healthy babies? Martinus explains this in an interesting and surprising way, which we shall now look at.

When artificial insemination can take place it is primarily due to the enormous abundance that characterizes many biological processes. There is such a surplus supply of the necessary things present that just a fraction is enough to make the process succeed. An example of this abundance could be the millions of sperm cells that are present in one portion of sperm, and only one is needed.

Martinus has explained how artificial insemination can take place in an article published in Kosmos 7, 1985. He writes: *"Any normal life process occurs in such an abundance that its mission can be fulfilled to a certain extent even if not all external conditions are present. The main condition for fertilization is the introduction of the male sperm into the female sexual organism. During the discharge of the sperm from the male sexual organism so much energy of bliss can be released, even if this discharge takes place artificially without intercourse with a female partner, that it can attract the aura of a discarnate being and thus create a connection or contact with it, a contact that can keep for a certain limited time or as long as the sperm can be kept artificially alive.... The talents of the discarnate spirit for the creation of an organism can thus, via the created connection and together with the organic creative force of the womb, come to expression and the embryogenesis begins. But it must be pointed out and noticed that this is an exception from the norm, through which a certain minus arises in this embryogenesis, viz. that the generations of this offspring will die out, as they gradually lose the ability to reproduce and thus become infertile".*

The conclusion is that in every case where there is a possibility for a physical incarnation to be initiated, a spiritual being will incarnate (there may even be a queue up there on the spiritual plane). But because of the *"minus that arises in this embryogenesis"* the being will be born with a reduced capacity for reproduction.

Children that have been conceived artificially quite simply do not have the same capacity for reproduction as children conceived in the normal way. Interestingly, this aspect has been confirmed via an investigation carried out by a group of scientists at Rigshospitalets Klinik for Vækst og Reproduktion (Clinic for Growth and Reproduction of the National Danish Hospital, Copenhagen) and Syddansk Universitet (University of Southern Denmark). The group of scientists has checked the sperm quality in a group of 1925 conscripts, of which 47 had been conceived artificially with some kind of help from the medical profession. All these 47 young men had a considerably lower sperm quality than the rest of the group. On average they had a sperm concentration (number of sperm cells per milliliter sperm) that was 46 % less than the rest of the group, and their sperm count (the amount of sperm cells in a single portion of sperm) was 45 % less. Their testicles were also smaller than those of the other conscripts. The young men that had been artificially conceived were simply not as fertile as those who had been conceived the normal way.

So, artificial insemination can take place in spite of the fact that it is not a totally natural process, but it comes with a "price tag". The price is a reduced reproductive capacity in the offspring.

Why Can't We Remember Our Past Lives?

Martinus has often been asked this question and every time he answers something like this.

We should be happy that we cannot remember our past lives, because these memories would to a high degree be confusing and disturbing in our present incarnation and for our project this time around. It is a blessing that we are not to be burdened with a number of day-conscious memories from former incarnations, because these would have an adverse effect in our present life.

This aspect is confirmed by the research of Dr. Ian Stevenson. Dr. Ian Stevenson, professor of psychiatry at the University of Virginia, USA, has for more than five decades gathered data from children that can remember a past life (15). Today Stevenson is in his eighties, but he is still researching. He has found approximately 3000 cases of children that spontaneously remember past lives, in many cases lives as identifiable persons. His cases have been gathered from countries all over the world, such as USA, Brazil, India, the Lebanon and Sri Lanka.

In practically all Stevenson's cases the very vivid memories from a past life were a considerable strain on the child. As soon as the child learned to speak, it would claim to have a different name than the one the parents called it, it would claim to have other parents, to live somewhere else, to have its own wife and children. It would also want to be taken to its real home. These memories meant that it was difficult for the child to settle into its present incarnation, and for the parents it would be very disconcerting to hear their child say such things.

When it is at all possible for some children to remember past lives, it is most probably an unintended manifestation and in general "not meant to be". We are not meant to actively remember our past incarnations. It turns out that the children that remember their past lives in most cases have "made the transition" under violent circumstances. They have either been murdered, killed or perished under great duress. It must be these intense experiences that leave such vivid memory traces that they "tag along" into the next incarnation.

However, it is normally so that the children forget these memories from past lives as they grow up — most of them will have forgotten most already around the age of eight.

We are not meant to remember our past lives actively. But then, on the other hand, we shouldn't go around thinking that we don't carry our past lives with us into each and every new incarnation. Our past lives are with us by virtue of our whole personality, our abilities, habits, tastes and tendencies, our morals and level of intelligence, what we can accept and be willing to do, what we find it in our hearts to do to others, what we dare or are afraid of, our possible phobias and, of course, our talents. Our talents, what we are good at, tell us with great accuracy what we have been up to in former lives. The person we are today is a direct result of what we have been doing in our past lives. Who we are today is a direct result of our accumulation of experience from former lives. We are quite simply a direct result of our former incarnations.

5. After Death

Death is only an imagined contrast to life. There is no real death understood as a cessation of consciousness and existence.

"...this, that some people think that we can die in the sense that we are obliterated and cease to be able to experience and create, is the biggest superstition that exists. There is no such death." (Martinus: "Death and Man's Mental World", Kosmos 4, 1992).

What we understand as death, and which many people nourish a completely unfounded fear of, is nothing but an exchange of bodies. An exchange of bodies means that our consciousness shifts from being carried by the physical body to being carried by the spiritual body. Our "I" and consciousness are just as alive without a physical body as with a physical body.

When our physical body is worn, be it because of illness, injury, wear and tear or old age, our consciousness shifts to one of our so-called spiritual bodies. These spiritual bodies surround our physical body and they consist of non-physical, ray-formed matter, which, as already mentioned, is a form of electromagnetic radiation.

A Corpse Is a Worn-out Instrument

As mentioned, our spiritual bodies, which exist in ray-formed matter, "sit" in a sort of bubble around the physical body. When the physical body is worn out, it has to be discarded, as it is no longer a useful instrument for the "I". During the process that we call death, the spiritual body withdraws from the physical body, which then becomes a corpse. So, a corpse is a useless instrument that has been discarded by the spirit, and from which the force or electricity, inherent in the ray-formed body, has been pulled out. Because ray-formed matter contains force or electricity, it is clear that a corpse is motionless, quite simply because it has now been cut off from its source of energy. This is actually analogous to a machine that has been disconnected from the power supply. Just as the hand mixer cannot whip cream when it has been unplugged, the body cannot move, when the electrical field of the spiritual body has pulled out. In both cases there is no current.

As the physical ingredients are totally identical in a living organism and in a corpse, it is obvious that what enlivens the body must be of a non-physical nature. Both a living organism and a corpse have brain, heart, lungs, liver, kidneys, intestines, blood vessels, cartilage, skeleton, hair, skin etc. so it is obvious that what gives life, movement and speech must be of a non-physical nature. What we call life is of an electrical nature.

And in the same way as the electricity still exists when we turn off the lamp, the spiritual body also exists, even though it is no longer connected to a physical body. At the onset of death the spiritual body withdraws from the now useless instrument, but as consciousness and the "I" are carried by the spiritual bodies, the actual living being, existing in ray-formed matter, will be just as alive and capable of experience as it was before. In its spiritual body, which is an electrical reality operating on a specific wavelength, it is now attracted to wavelengths in the spiritual world. So also on the other side of "death" the law of attraction is the most important natural law.

We Are Our Vibration

Just as it is our joint vibrational standard with its matching wavelength that determines which parents we are born to, it is our vibration that determines our fate after death. In the same way as we are, on the earthly plane, attracted to people, societies, organizations etc. that we are on wavelength with, our "I" after its separation from the physical body, is attracted to wavelengths on the spiritual plane that match our own wavelength. This "locating" or "finding one's place" in the spiritual world takes place automatically based on the law of attraction. If our spiritual body vibrates on a wavelength of e.g. 101,5 FM, well, then our destination is 101,5 FM in the spiritual world. It is law.

"Life after death shapes itself according to the mentality of the person, his moral and intellectual standard"
"When people think about death, and they in their consciousness leave the possibility open that there can be a life after this, then the next thought will be: how will such a life unfold? And the answer must be: the unfolding and experience of life, which a human being is subject to, when he or she has left the physical organism, shapes itself according to the way of thinking, habits, beliefs and the moral and intellectual standard of the being. That which in particular has filled the consciousness of the being, while he or she lived in the physical world, will also characterize life after the being has left this world. The thoughts of a human being are nothing tangible, indeed, there are people who say: "Thoughts are nothing, you know". But that is a huge misapprehension. It is true that thoughts are intangible, when they are not manifested in physical creation, but still they are there and they are something essential in Man." (Martinus: "Death and Man's Mental World", Kosmos 4, 1992, my underling added).

We should not go around believing that just because we are "dead", then we are no longer the same. When we pull our "I" out of the physical body, this "I" is exactly the same as before. And it is on the basis of the standard of this "I" that we "are placed" in the spiritual world. What our consciousness holds of thoughts, abilities, habits and beliefs will be our point of attraction when we are "placed" in the spiritual world.

"When people begin to understand that their life in the physical world is a life in a materialized world of thoughts, their attitude to spiritual problems will gradually change, and thus also their attitude to the so-called death. But people are still so used to believing that thoughts do not mean anything, "thoughts are duty-free", we say, and then the truth is that people, both through the process of transformation from the spiritual to the physical world, i.e. the birth or the incarnation, and through the transformation from the physical to the spiritual world, the so-called death, must "pay duty" of their thoughts, as their fate in both the physical and the spiritual world depends on their way of thinking". (Martinus: "Death and Man's Mental World", Kosmos 4, 1992, my underling added).

We must "pay duty" of our thoughts, says Martinus. By this he means that it is our joint thought climate that decides where we "land" in the spiritual world. It is self-evident that a being, whose thoughts are filled with hatred, revenge and killing, has a consciousness that vibrates on a different wavelength than that of a being whose thoughts are filled with altruism, unconditional love and a desire to help others. It would be just as impossible for the two to "land" at the same destination (wavelength) in the spiritual world, as it would be unthinkable that they would both belong to the organization "Peace on Earth" here on our plane. Their vibrations and wavelengths are at two different ends of the scale, so they must necessarily be placed accordingly. It is law.

The Unpleasant Good

As already mentioned the goal of our development on the physical plane is to become "Man in the image and likeness of God". Such a human being radiates love to everybody and everything and lives to serve others. He or she has completely erased any type of animal way of thinking and his or her mentality has been totally cleansed from all types of intolerance, selfishness, possession, greed, jealousy, anger, irritation, slander, self-promotion and desire for personal power. It is obvious that such a being cannot participate in the killing of other living beings and consequently he or she does not take meat or blood products as nourishment, but lives solely on a vegetarian diet.

It is obvious that the development towards this high goal takes many, many incarnations. The way of thinking of some people is still very much influenced by animal mentality, and often they are living in the heart of darkness, where they reap war, terrorism, killings, accidents and natural disasters. This may seem very tragic, but it is actually "an unpleasant good", says Martinus. It is good in the sense that the war, the accidents and the sufferings are instrumental in cleansing the animal mentality from our thought sphere. Each suffering we are subject to will make us more humane, compassionate and all-loving. The sufferings are "cosmic sources of wisdom". With each incarnation on the physical plane we "move forward" towards becoming real human beings in the image of God and with each incarnation more wisdom is "built into" the beings.

We can say that the mission of the physical world is to constitute a place where our mentality can be cleansed, refined and "polished".

But couldn't we "just" learn that in the spiritual world? No, says Martinus, because in the spiritual world there is no suffering, and as it is a light and refined world of thoughts, it is not a good place to learn to think and act in the right way. There is simply too little resistance. But here on the physical plane we get our own actions back on the strength of the law of karma, and it is through this "life's own speech" that we really learn to adjust our behavior.

"Human beings incarnate here in the physical world in order to learn to think logically i.e. to think in accordance with the laws of life. When they don't do that, they think wrongly, and in the physical world "it hurts" to think wrongly".

You Do not Develop Morally and Intellectually in the Spiritual Worlds

"The fact that "it hurts" to think in discord with the laws of life, will gradually make the human beings try to think along other lines than the ones that created suffering and pain; their attitude to life and their way of life changes. But couldn't the beings learn this in the spiritual world? No, they can't, in the spiritual world there is no suffering and pain. There can be some in the intermediate state or during the very first time after the being has left its physical body and this is just because this state is actually a part of the physical world, where the beings are imprisoned by their own materialistic way of thinking. They are freed from this by the guardian angels when they ask for help, and after that they experience their cycle through the spiritual spheres, and their experiences there depend on what their consciousness holds of purely humane thinking."

(Martinus: "Death and Man's Mental World", Kosmos 4, 1992, my underling added).

In the spiritual world there is no suffering and pain. This means that the spiritual world can be viewed as a "holiday and leisure resort" away from the trials and tribulations of the physical world.

"For that reason the passage of the being through the physical process of death actually becomes a passage from a large and very heavy field of operation to a field of experience, which in itself in comparison with the

physical, must be viewed as a field of rest". (Martinus: "The Road to Paradise", booklet 25, chapter 24).

We don't progress in our development on the spiritual plane, so also in that respect it is a period of rest. It is furthermore a period of rest, where we are allowed to experience so much light, happiness and joy as we have come to "deserve". Our experiences on the spiritual plane *"depend on what our consciousness holds of purely humane thinking."* This means that we will experience a realm of happiness and light that is directly related to the strength or quality of our humane development. For that reason each and every one of us will get an individual experience of paradise, completely based on the degree of refinement of our humanity. We can "only" get as "high" as our best sides have been developed. With each physical incarnation our humanity is developed, and this means that we, in each period of rest, can step up one grade higher than where we "stood" the last time we were "dead".

Destinations in the Spiritual World

We can imagine the spiritual world as a hierarchically constructed sphere, consisting of wavelengths spanning from fairly coarse, "animal" wavelengths to very fine, humane and altruistic wavelengths. There are wavelengths that correspond to every imaginable form of thought climate. There are, in truth,"many mansions in the house of the father". A wavelength can be imagined as a landscape of thought matter created by all the beings, whose mentalities vibrate with enough similarity to attract each other. The joint thought matter of these "likeminded" beings creates a kind of "landscape", which is experienced as an outer world by the spiritual being. It is to such a "landscape" that we are drawn, when we leave our physical body. And the landscape to which we are drawn will be a match to our own thought sphere – the law of attraction sees to that. This means that the artist will be drawn to a landscape where art prevails, the musician will be drawn to a wonderful world of music, the intellectual person will be drawn to a world of studies and science etc. Also the animals are attracted to wavelengths that correspond to their consciousness, and it means that they will experience a "landscape" with ideal habitats and living conditions that correspond to their level of development.

Logically, it also means that the suicide bomber will be attracted to a wavelength that corresponds to the thought climate, which dominated his or her mentality when the bomb was brought to explosion. If the dominating thoughts were of hatred, revenge and murder, well, then it is to such a wavelength that the spirit of the suicide bomber is attracted. Such a wavelength will be dark, somber and full of hatred, as it will consist of thoughts of hatred, revenge and war – a "landscape" constructed by the thought climates of beings that are on wavelength with war, hatred, revenge and murder. Not an attractive destination at all.

But even the suicide bomber's stay in this hateful "landscape" will only last as long as he or she wants it. The moment help is asked for, help will be provided, so that the being can exit the dark wavelength. But, of course, one has to know that it helps to ask for help. But sooner or later the being on the dark wavelength will become so unhappy, that he or she asks for help. And then help will come in the shape of one's guardian angels that will help one exit the somber wavelength and enter a lighter one that corresponds to the most developed and most humane part of one's psyche.

"As humanity represents beings from many different stages of development, and these beings differ from each other with respect to knowledge, intelligence and attitude to life, their dreams and wishes or ideal lives will be correspondingly different. The spiritual world can be divided in corresponding spheres or areas of experience. In this way these areas constitute a scale of steps for the experience of life, ranging from the sphere of the savage human being to the area of "the perfect human being in the image of God". Every step has its specific wavelengths, and it is by virtue of these that the manifestation of the beings in question is released. As the highest manifestation on the steps is the ideal or most desired existence of the beings, and these existences again are the experience of paradise of the beings, it becomes clear that various forms of paradise exist. The beings on the various steps each gets its specific form of paradise corresponding to their mental state and concept of life". (Martinus: "The Road to Paradise", booklet no. 25, chapter 42).

As every single being, due to the law of attraction, is "classified" according to the most developed part of their mentality, such a "classification" will be experienced as the culmination of bliss, wellbeing and joy. Indeed, paradise is no illusion. And there are as many forms of paradise as there are mental states and concepts of life. Each and every individual paradise will be experienced as the culmination of bliss – the culmination of our own individual perception of what bliss is. It doesn't get any better than that.

Spiritual Matter Shapes Itself According to Our Thoughts

The spiritual world is a very light field of operation in comparison to the physical world, which is a heavy field of operation. The type of matter, of which the spiritual world consists, is ray-formed or electromagnetic radiation, and this means that it shapes itself according to our thoughts through the law of attraction. As easy as it is for us physical beings to "change thoughts" from thinking of a palm clad tropical island to thinking of a snow-covered alpine top, just as easy is it for the spiritual being to "go visiting" in the spiritual spheres.

Whatever the being thinks about will manifest before him as an outer, figurative reality. We can "travel" in the thought to any destination of our desires and we can "meet up" with the beings that we have known and loved in former incarnations.

"The joy of being together with other people that we are on wavelength with can be great already here in the physical world, and yet it is nothing compared to the joy and altruistic love that we will feel emanating from the beings in the spiritual worlds. Music, art and science are specific thought climates, which everybody, who has an interest in these fields, can get on wavelength with on the spiritual plane in such a concentrated form, as their consciousness can take. You don't learn anything new in the spiritual worlds in the sense that you develop morally and intellectually, but you discover that you can make use of the abilities, you have developed in the physical world, to a larger extent and with immediate effect. You think, and then the thoughts appear as pictures in spiritual matter. The spiritual bodies of the beings also consist of thought matter, and for that reason it is no problem if people, who have known and loved each other, can recognize each other in the spiritual world. They can, and when they think of each other, they will meet, and they will appear to each other in a shape that resembles the one in which they knew each other in the physical world, even though the spiritual body will be more beautiful." (Martinus: "Death and Man's Mental World", Kosmos 4, 1992, my underling added).

Weeding in the Thought Sphere

Death is a wonderful, paradisiacal period of rest, so it is completely unnecessary to have any kind of fear for this passage. There is only reason to look forward to this "five star holiday" that death can be seen as. But in order to secure a "better room" at the luxury hotel, it is a good idea that you, while you are here on the physical plane, make an effort to "weed out" your mental sphere. The better your mix of thoughts is, the better will you be placed. It means that you can actively work on weeding out "low" thought climates, such as all kinds of dishonesty, jealousy, envy, slander, self-promotion, lying, boasting, stealing, greed, enmity, hatred, gossip etc. The more your mentality is filled with altruism, unselfishness, self-sacrifice, kindness and love, the better will your experience in the spiritual world be. And then there is less to weed out in the next incarnation.

"It is while you live on the physical plane that you must work on developing your mental world

"There is no reason to fear death, which leads the human being into a wonderful and light world of thought, but there is every reason to work with the development of your own world of thought, while you are living on the physical plane, as you thus create bigger and better possibilities for what life in the spiritual worlds can bring you, at the same time as you create better possibilities for what the next physical incarnation can bring of experiences and further development." (Martinus: "Death and Man's Mental World", Kosmos 4, 1992).

The Road of Life

Let us here at the end take pleasure in what Martinus says in the following quotation:

"We have thus reached the end of the road with this our short overview of the road of life or the road to paradise. Through the mentioned overview we have obtained a small insight into the reason why the beings for a time necessarily must live in two worlds, the spiritual world, which is the primary world and the home of the experience of life and creation of all living beings, and in the physical world, which is a vital added sphere, whose material is the very matter for God's creation of the living beings' transformation to become like him. Without this matter, all creation of consciousness would, as we have seen, be impossible. For that reason it is a life condition for the living beings for a time to incarnate in this matter, in order to experience, as also pointed out earlier, how their behavior must be and how it mustn't be, in order that they can thus be perfected in the experience and practice of this: to be one with God. The reincarnations or the long series of physical lives on Earth of the beings thus become visible as God's huge and wide highway towards his own brilliant and eternal paradise on the highest pinnacles of all-wisdom, altruism and omnipotence. Here in this all-outshining, highest paradise we are at the final goal for all life's movement towards the pinnacles of light or the eternal father. There is no living being in the physical universe that is not on this road that leads to this, the divine home of all beings. This, the road of life, is exceedingly long, but we have seen that good care is taken of the tired wanderer, who has to pass it. There are many inns here that have been built in the same style of joy and happiness as the home of the Father or God's own paradise, which is the goal of all the travelers that walk along this divine road. Here the needy, wandering son of God can spend the night, rest and enjoy all the warmth and wellbeing of the fatherly love. Here he can have his worn and decrepit physical "vehicle" exchanged, indeed he can have a completely new travel equipment, so that he can, refreshed and with new spirits, again start out on a new stage to the next inn and so forth from inn to inn on the long journey towards the great revelation of the adventure of life or the solution to the mystery of life or the enigma of the

universe. The physical lives on Earth are the living being's stages of the walk between the inns. The inns are the same as the living being's spiritual lives or sojourns in paradise between its physical lives on Earth. We have already seen what these paradises mean to the living being. Here it is allowed, for a while, to unburden itself of the heavy, mental burdens, sorrows, worries, sufferings and hardships of the travel equipment and be dressed in its heavenly, princely attire: the halo of peace, joy, happiness and light, at the same time as it is allowed to live in the fulfillment of its highest wishes.   And after thus having dwelled in the love of the father and having had its zest for life renewed and achieved new, divine strength, a new physical organism or vehicle, the eternal son of God can again set out on a new journey in the physical world and cover the stage to the fatherly blessing of the next inn". (Martinus: "The Road to Paradise", booklet no. 25, chapter 56).

Death Is an Illusion

There is no death. What we perceive as death is only an imagined contrast to life. No living being can die. We can lose our physical instrument, but not life itself. The existence of our "I" is not dependent on a physical instrument. Our "I" is as alive without the physical instrument as it was with it. We are eternal beings on a never-ending journey through physical and spiritual realms. After a lifetime on the physical plane, we need a rest from the trials and tribulations of the physical world, and such a rest is an experience of our own particular paradise. When we have rested and are ready for new experiences, then we reincarnate into a new little body, made to our own specifications, and we continue with our development from where we "let go" the last time we were incarnated. For each life we live, we are shaped and molded towards becoming "Man in the image and likeness of God". We are all subject to this process of perfection. We are all on our way and everything is very good.

You can read more about Martinus´ work and world picture in my books: Death Is an Illusion, The Beginning is Near, The Undiscovered Country and The Downfall of Marriage. You can find all my books on my website: www.newspiritualscience.com

6. Supplement

26 Affirmations

These affirmations can be practiced as often as needed and are guaranteed to work. Sit down quietly for 15 minutes each day in the morning and concentrate on an affirmation of your choice. Repeat the affirmation during the day whenever you have a quiet moment. The next day you can repeat the process or move on to another affirmation of your choice.

1

I am an extension of source energy. I matter

I am an important part of something that is much bigger than myself. I matter to myself and to others. I am a significant person with incredible potential and abilities. I appreciate myself. I love myself.

2

I create my own reality through my thoughts

My thoughts are magnetic and with them I attract the people, circumstances and conditions of my life. Thoughts become things. Therefore I choose only good thoughts.

3

My thoughts are the key to my happiness.

I choose my thoughts carefully, because what I focus on and what manifests is always a match. Every time. No exceptions. Positive thoughts bring positive circumstances, people and events. I only think positive thoughts.

4

As I think, I vibrate, as I vibrate I attract

My thoughts vibrate on a certain wavelength. With the wavelength of my thoughts, I attract similar wavelengths. My point of attraction is my predominant thought. My predominant thoughts are positive and happy, so I attract only positive and happy people, circumstances and occurrences.

5

I take full responsibility for my life

I have created my life through the thoughts I have thought. My life is my own making. I have nobody else to blame for my health, my finances, my circumstances or my happiness. I am the only one responsible.

6

I listen to my emotional guidance system

I listen to my emotional guidance system. If a thought feels bad, I avoid it and replace it with a thought that feels good. I think only thoughts that feel good. How life feels is what life is.

7

I care how I feel

It is important to me that I feel good. I choose to focus only on things that make me feel good. I know that feeling good is the fountain of youth, the river of wellness, the stream of abundance, the way to all things that are important to me.

8

I am in control of my feelings

I am in control of my feelings. I confront negative feelings. I only reach out for desirable feelings of kindness, joy, happiness and love. I am strong, balanced and controlled. I am in charge of my emotions. They don't control me.

9

I care about my vibration

I know that my vibration, based on the thoughts I choose to think, is my point of attraction. I realize that I cannot attract anything that is not in vibrational alignment with my own vibration. Therefore I focus on abundance, contentment and happiness. I focus on what is right, bright and beautiful. I see the best in every situation and in every person.

10

I am powerful!

I can because I think I can. I can do anything. My belief system is limitless. I am powerful. I am not afraid to walk new roads. I am a person of great potential.

11

I am grateful!

I live in gratitude. I count my blessing every day. I am grateful for what I have attracted into my life. I choose to focus only on what is good and full of bliss. I enjoy the good life. There is within me an invincible summer.

12

I am happy!

I understand that if I am going to be happy it is up to me. I do not rely on others to make me happy and I don't expect that they will. The message is: I am good, I am happy. I won't be hard on myself and I have made peace with where I am.

13

My mind is positive today

My mind is positive today. I fill it with positive thoughts only. I am not an "against" person, but I am "for" anything that is uplifting, joyful and positive. I feed my mind with positive aspects only. I choose only to attract joy, happiness and bliss.

14

I deactivate negative thoughts

If a negative thought crops up, I immediately deactivate it by replacing it with a positive thought. There are millions of thoughts available. I have a free choice, so I choose only happy thoughts that lift my spirit and give my imagination wings.

15

I live and let live

I am no control freak. I have let loose of my need to control others. They should do as they please, just as I do as I please. I do not need others to make me happy. I make myself happy through my ability to focus on the positive. I seek to please myself. Only then can I be of service to others.

16

I only treat people as I would want to be treated

I know that what I do to others I eventually do to myself, due to the law of cause and effect. I only treat others the way I would like to be treated myself. If somebody treats me badly, I just shrug, because I know that they will be treated the same way by the universe. I don't have to do anything.

17

I anticipate with joy and expectation

I know that the things I desire will come to me quickly when I anticipate their coming with joy and expectation. I only focus on abundance and plenty. I am so looking forward to the next day of my life.

18

I am healthy

I have perfect health because I focus only on health. I see myself as fit, strong, healthy and able all through life. I will always have my ideal weight. I will always look good, because good looks come from within.

19

I follow my bliss

It matters not what other people think of me or my doings. I go where my heart takes me. Because I follow my bliss I am tuned in, tapped in, turned on. Everything that I desire comes to me because I follow my bliss.

20

I don't have to get it right

I don't blame myself or others for my life. I did the best I could and if the result did not turn out quite right, I can redo it. I am an eternal being, so there is all the time in the world to get things right.

21

I forgive

I forgive myself for what I have done just as I forgive others for what they have done. I move on from things that happened in the past – I don't live there. I live in the now and here I have my point of attraction. I only attract what is good, positive and joyful. The past doesn't matter.

22

I think big!

I think big. I wish big. My imagination is limitless. I will accomplish my wildest dreams. I will focus on what I most want. I only see possibilities. I don't have to know how my dreams will come true. The how is the domain of the universe.

23

I am a genius at focusing

I focus only on the positive and on things I like and appreciate. It doesn't bother me that undesirable things exist in the world – as long as I don't focus on them, they do not worry me.

24

I am a magnet to money

I am a magnet to money. I will achieve my success through providing service to others. Everything healthy that I desire is on its way towards me right now. Everything I touch turns to gold.

25

I count my blessing every day

I count my blessing every day. I realize how fortunate I am. I do not take anything for granted. I am richly blessed and I am thankful for this fact. Things are going great for me.

26

I am a worthy person

I am a worthy person. I have a strong sense of worth regardless of what anyone says about me, thinks of me or does to me. I don't have to prove anything or "be anybody". I am free for the desperate need for approval. I am of worth. I matter.

About the author

Else Byskov was a searching soul until, in 1995, she came across the work of Martinus, the Danish visionary and mystic. She found the work absolutely fascinating and thought that she had to tell the world about it. Today she has studied the amazing spiritual revelations of Martinus for 21 years and she is an international top authority on his work. She has written 5 books about aspects of Martinus´ revelations. Else was born in Denmark and she has university degrees in Spanish and English philology. For many years she worked as a teacher and translator / interpreter. Today she lives in Southern Spain. She is a passionate hiker (and author of 3 hiking books) and a vegetarian (and author of a vegetarian cook book).

Please visit Else´s new website www.newspiritualscience.com

From there you can download free samples of her other books, articles and audios. You can watch videos on central themes in Martinus´ teachings and you can read her blog. You can read interesting facts about Martinus and see some of his symbols. You can also subscribe to Else´s newsletters by downloading chapters from one of her books and entering your email address.

Please also like her Facebook page New Spiritual Science and see the amazing quotes that she uploads every day

https://www.facebook.com/Newspiritualscience.101/

If you have liked this book, Else would really appreciate if you would be so kind as to write a review on Amazon.com
https://www.amazon.com/Art-Attraction-New-Aspects-Law/dp/1461092388/ref=sr_1_5?s=books&ie=UTF8&qid=1467801585&sr=1-5&keywords=Else+Byskov

Thank you!

Else has 2 other websites:

www.deathisanillusion.dk
www.elsebyskov.com (hiking)

Feel free to contact Else on
else@newspiritualscience.com with questions or comments.

You can visit the website of The Martinus Institute at
www.martinus.dk
Here you can read parts of Martinus´ original work online and see which books have been translated into English and many other languages.

7. Notes

1. The small holding of Moskildvad, situated at the outskirts of Sindal, in the northern part of Jutland, Denmark, has since 1990 been a kind of museum to Martinus. The house has been re-built and re-decorated to look the way it did, when Martinus lived there. It is open to the public and can be visited during the summer months. The address is: Moskildvad, Ulstedbovej 15, 9870 Sindal, Denmark.

2. All translations from Danish into English are by Else Byskov.

3. Cosmic consciousness. I have taken the following definition of cosmic consciousness from Dr. Richard Bucke's book "Cosmic Consciousness" from 1901: *"The prime characteristic of cosmic consciousness is, as the name implies, a consciousness of the cosmos – that is of the life and order of the universe....Along with the consciousness of the cosmos there occurs an intellectual enlightenment or illumination, which alone would place the individual on a new plane of existence – would make him almost a member of a new species. To this is added a state of moral exaltation, an indescribable feeling of elevation and joyousness, and a quickening of the moral sense, which is fully as striking and more important both to the individual and to the race than is the enhanced intellectual power. With these come what may be called a sense of immortality, a consciousness of eternal life, not a conviction that he shall have this, but the consciousness that he has it already".*

4. The following books can be read as an introduction to Martinus' world picture: In English: Else Byskov: "Death Is an Illusion", Paragon House Publishers, USA 2002. In German: Else Byskov: "Der Tod ist eine Illusion", Martinus Verlag, 2006. In Spanish: "La muerte es una Ilusion". Else Byskov: The Beginning Is Near" (Create Space, 2015).

5. See for instance: Jane Roberts: "Seth Speaks", Bantam Books, 1972, "The Early Sessions", 1997 , 8-10 volumes. For a complete list of books on Seth see: http://www.spiritual-endeavors.org/seth/books.htm

6. See: http://www.abraham-hicks.com/ for a complete list of publications.

7. See for instance Michael Talbot: "The Holographic Universe", page 91.

8. The example is mentioned in both Talbot and Siegler. See the bibliography.

9. The example is from "The Secret".

10. Abraham hardly mentions the subject of karma, so there are no references to the Abraham material in this chapter.

11. See http://www.scotese.com/climate.htm)

12. The much publicized claim that the climate has become warmer is now being questioned by a group of 100 scientists from the most prominent universities of the planet. The scientists claim that there has been no net warming since 1998, as certain areas of the planet has experienced much colder winters as usual. Furthermore the group claims that the changes observed fall within the natural limits of heating and cooling over the last 10.000 years. Please see the impressive list of signers and their arguments on: www.nationalpost.com/news/story.html?id=164002

13. See Per Bruus-Jensen: "Martinus Kosmologi – en kort præsentation", page 71, Nordisk Impuls.

14. In the book "The Ideal Food" Martinus explains what is the correct nourishment for us humans at our present stage of development. For most of us meat products will constitute too coarse a diet with too strong a vibration, which it is very detrimental to our organism to process and digest. For that reason Martinus recommends a vegetarian diet, supplemented by milk. All types of alcoholic beverages are totally foreign to the human organism and should be avoided, as should the intake of tobacco and drugs.

15. See the bibliography for a list of Ian Stevenson's publications.

8. Bibliography

<u>Dooley, Mike:</u> "Notes from the Universe", TUT's Enterprises, Inc. 2005

<u>Hicks, Esther and Jerry:</u>

Books:
"Ask and it is Given", Hay House Inc. 2004
"The Law of Attraction", Hay House Inc. 2006
"The Amazing Power of Deliberate Intent", Hay House Inc. 2006

CDs:
"The Law of Attraction" set of 5 CDs, Hay House Inc.
"Money and Manifestation", Abraham-Hicks Publications, 2005.
"The Astonishing Power of Emotions", 2007.

DVDs:
"The Secret behind the Secret", Hay House Inc. 2007.
"The Law of Attraction in Action, episode 1", Hay House, Inc. 2007.
"Abraham Alaskan Well-Being Cruise 2005", Abraham-Hicks Publications.

<u>Martinus:</u>
"Livets Bog" 7 bind, Borgens Forlag, København, 1932-1960.
"Det evige verdensbillede" 4 bind, Borgens Forlag, København 1987-1994.
"Logik" , 1987.
"Bisættelse", ("On Funerals"), Borgens Forlag, København, 1951.
"Artikelsamling 1", ("Collection of Articles 1")Borgens Forlag, København, 2002.
"Den intellektualiserede kristendom", ("The Intellectualized Christianity"),
Borgens Forlag, København, 2004.

Booklets:
1. "Menneskehedens skæbne" ("The Fate of Mankind")
2. "Påske" ("Easter")
3. "Hvad er sandhed" ("What is Truth?")
4. "Omkring min missions fødsel" ("On the Birth of my Mission")
5. "Den ideelle føde" ("The Ideal Food")
6. "Blade af Guds billedbog" ("Pages of God's Picture Book")
7. "Den længst levende afgud" ("The Longest Living Idol")
8. "Mennesket og verdensbilledet" ("Mankind and the World Picture")

9. "Mellem to verdensepoker" ("Between Two World Epochs")
10. "Kosmisk bevidsthed" ("Cosmic Consciousness")
11. "Bønnens mysterium" ("The Mystery of Prayer")
12. "Vejen til indvielse" ("The Road to Initiation")
13. "Juleevangeliet" ("The Gospel of Christmas")
14. "Bevidsthedens skabelse" ("The Creation of Consciousness")
15. "Ud af mørket" ("Out of Darkness")
16. "Reinkarnationsprincippet" ("The Principle of Reincarnation")
17. "Verdensreligion og verdenspolitik" ("World Religion and World Politics")
18. "Livets skæbnespil" ("The Fate Drama of Life")
19. "Kosmiske glimt" ("Cosmic Glimpses")
20. "Meditation" ("Meditation")
21. "Hinsides dødsfrygten" ("Beyond the Fear of Death")
22. "Livets vej" ("The Road of Life")
23. "De levende væseners udødelighed" ("The Immortality of the Living Beings")
24. "Kulturens skabelse" ("The Creation of Culture")
25. "Vejen til Paradis" ("The Road to Paradise")
26. "Djævlebevidsthed og Kristusbevidsthed" ("Devil Mentality and Christ Mentality")
27. "Verdensfredens skabelse" ("The Creation of World Peace")
28. "To slags kærlighed" ("Two Kinds of Love")

The monthly magazine "Kosmos" 1989 – 2007, published by Martinus Institute.

Samarbejdsstrukturen" ("The Structure for Cooperation"), Martinus Institute, Copenhagen, 1992.

"Gennem dødens port – søvnen og døden" ("Through the Gates of Death – Sleep and Death", leaflet), Martinus Institute.

"Vejen til den sande lykke" ("The Road to True Happiness", leaflet), Martinus Institute.

Martinus' Erindringer" ("The Memoirs of Martinus"), Zinglersens Forlag, Copenhagen, 1987.

Peale, Norman Vincent: "The Power of Positive Thinking", 1953

Radin, Dean: "The Conscious Universe", Harper Edge, New York, 1997

Siegel, Bernie S.: "Love, Medicine and Miracles", 1986

Stevenson, Dr. Ian:
"Twenty Cases Suggestive of Reincarnation", University Press of Virginia, Charlottesville 1974.
"Where Reincarnation and Biology Intersect", Praeger, Westport, 1997.

Talbot, Michael: "The Holographic Universe", Harper Perennial, New York, 1991

The Secret (DVD)

Stephensen, Birgit: "Aura og Farver", Borgen, København 1989.

Made in the USA
Las Vegas, NV
09 December 2021

36880563R00094